Beyond
Conversations
About Race

A Guide for Discussions With Students, Teachers, and Communities

Washington Collado
Sharroky Hollie
Rosa Isiah
Yvette Jackson
Anthony Muhammad
Douglas Reeves
Kenneth C. Williams

Solution Tree | Press
a division of
Solution Tree

555 North Morton Street
Bloomington, IN 47404
800.733.6786 (toll free) / 812.336.7700
FAX: 812.336.7790

email: info@SolutionTree.com
SolutionTree.com

Printed in the United States of America

Library of Congress Cataloging-in-Publication Data

Names: Collado, Washington, 1962- author. | Hollie, Sharroky, 1967- author.
    | Isiah, Rosa, author. | Jackson, Yvette, author. | Muhammad, Anthony,
    author. | Reeves, Douglas B., 1953 author. | Williams, Kenneth C.,
    author.
Title: Beyond conversations about race : a guide for discussions with
    students, teachers, and communities / Washington Collado, Sharroky
    Hollie, Rosa Isiah, Yvette Jackson, Anthony Muhammad, Douglas Reeves,
    Kenneth C. Williams.
Description: Bloomington, IN : Solution Tree Press, [2021] | Includes
    bibliographical references and index.
Identifiers: LCCN 2021013595 (print) | LCCN 2021013596 (ebook) | ISBN
    9781952812798 (paperback) | ISBN 9781952812804 (ebook)
Subjects: LCSH: Race--Study and teaching | Racism--Study and teaching |
    Race discrimination--Study and teaching.
Classification: LCC HT1506 .C65 2021 (print) | LCC HT1506 (ebook) | DDC
    305.80071--dc23
LC record available at https://lccn.loc.gov/2021013595
LC ebook record available at https://lccn.loc.gov/2021013596

Solution Tree
Jeffrey C. Jones, CEO
Edmund M. Ackerman, President

Solution Tree Press
President and Publisher: Douglas M. Rife
Associate Publisher: Sarah Payne-Mills
Art Director: Rian Anderson
Managing Production Editor: Kendra Slayton
Copy Chief: Jessi Finn
Production Editor: Rita Carlberg
Content Development Specialist: Amy Rubenstein
Proofreader: Evie Madsen
Text and Cover Designer: Rian Anderson
Compositor: Kelsey Hergül
Editorial Assistants: Sarah Ludwig and Elijah Oates

Acknowledgments

Solution Tree Press would like to thank the following reviewers:

Tonya Alexander
English Teacher (NBCT)
Owego Free Academy
Owego, New York

Daniel Coles
Senior Program Manager
The Morningside Center for
Teaching Social Responsibility
New York, New York

Lillie G. Jessie
Retired Principal of a Model
PLC School, School
   Board Member
Prince William County
   Public Schools
Manassas, Virginia

David Pillar
Assistant Director
Hoosier Hills Career Center
Bloomington, Indiana

Table of Contents

Chapter 14

How Can We Advocate for Change?

Chapter 15

Why Isn't Being Right Enough?

Chapter 16

How Do We Create Equity Consciousness?

Chapter 17

The Next Chapter: How Do We Shift From Opposing Bigotry to Practicing Anti-Racism?

About the Authors

 **Washington "Nino" Collado, PhD,** was born in the Dominican Republic in 1962 in a small town called Jánico and was raised surrounded by educators. His mother, María Tejada, and seven of his uncles and aunts were teachers. After the death of his mother in 1970, Dr. Collado and his three sisters traveled to the United States to live with their father in 1975. In New York, he started his studies in New York City Public Schools in the seventh grade and went on to Franklin K. Lane High School in Brooklyn, New York.

Dr. Collado began his career in education in 1986, teaching Spanish and English as a second language in New York City Public Schools. In 1992, he and his family moved to South Florida. While working in Broward County Public Schools' Multicultural Department, he developed curriculum and conducted trainings for teachers and administrators on multicultural education and community engagement.

Dr. Collado began his career in school administration as an assistant principal at Broward County Public Schools and was promoted to principal in 2005. Collectively, he has served fifteen years as principal at Lyons Creek Middle School, Marjory Stoneman Douglas High School, and, presently, James S. Rickards Middle School. He also served as president of the Broward Principals' and Assistants' Association (BPAA).

Throughout his career, Dr. Collado has devoted much of his time to teaching and orienting school leaders and educators. He has traveled to various countries and more than twenty U.S. states as a motivational speaker on matters of school leadership and family engagement. He has also served as a panelist at CNN en Español, Telemundo, Univision, and others. He has written more than one hundred articles for newspapers and magazines in New York and Florida, including the *Miami Herald*, and has published the following three books: *Parents, Don't Forget Your Homework*; *Padres, No Olviden su Tarea*; and *Liderazgo y Escuelas Efectivas*.

Sharroky Hollie, PhD, is a national educator who provides professional development to thousands of educators in the area of cultural responsiveness. Since 2000, Dr. Hollie has trained more than 150,000 educators and worked in nearly 2,000 classrooms.

Going back twenty-five years, he has been a classroom teacher at the middle and high school levels, a central office professional development coordinator in Los Angeles Unified School District, a school founder and administrator, and a university professor in teacher education at the Cal State University. Dr. Hollie has also been a visiting professor for Webster University in St. Louis and a guest lecturer at Stanford and UCLA.

In addition to his experience in education, he has authored several texts and journal articles. Most recently, he wrote *Strategies for Culturally and Linguistically Responsive Teaching and Learning* and contributed a chapter in the *Oxford Handbook of African American Language*.

Dr. Hollie's first book, *Culturally and Linguistically Responsive Teaching and Learning: Classroom Practices for Student Success* was published in 2011, followed soon thereafter by *The Will to Lead, the Skill to Teach*, cowritten with Dr. Anthony Muhammad. In 2003, he and two colleagues founded the Culture and Language Academy of Success, a laboratory school that demonstrated the principles of cultural responsiveness in an exemplary schoolwide model, which operated until 2013.

Rosa Isiah, EdD, is an educational leader, international speaker, leadership consultant, and author who currently serves her school community as the director of elementary schools, equity, and access at Norwalk-La Mirada Unified School District (NLMUSD) in California. As an educational practitioner, Dr. Isiah has also served as a teacher, bilingual specialist, language arts specialist, assistant principal, principal, and coordinator of federal and state programs.

Dr. Isiah is passionate about actionable equity and social justice in education. As principal for seven years at Smith Elementary School, she focused on supporting the development of a healthy school culture, building and sustaining a professional learning community, and meeting the academic and social-emotional needs of the whole child and whole community. Her school's data, as measured by the California state assessment and site data, demonstrates steady growth and the closing of achievement gaps for historically underserved students. Smith Elementary was recognized for closing gaps for African American, English learner, and Hispanic students. Dr. Isiah is proud of the growth and success of the Smith Elementary community and attributes that success to a focus on school culture, PLCs, equity in action, and a whole-community approach to teaching and learning.

Dr. Isiah is a connected educator and the founder of the #WeLeadEd Twitter chat. She is also the host of the *WeLeadED* Body and Mind (BAM) Radio podcast with a focus on leadership through a social justice and equity lens. Dr. Isiah was recognized as the 2016 BAM Education Radio Thought Leader of the Year and the Loyola Marymount University 2019 Educational Leader for Social Justice recipient. Dr. Isiah is the coauthor of three books focused on leadership, relationships, social and emotional learning, and equity: *FULLYCHARGED: 140 Battery Charging Maslow and Bloom Strategies for Students, Parents, and Staff; FULLYCHARGED Systems: Stories, Science, and Strategies to Skyrocket Success*; and *Education Write Now: Top Strategies for Improving Relationships and Culture*. She has also contributed her voice to leadership books, blogs, and panels on equity, anti-racism, leadership, school culture, and English learners.

Dr. Isiah holds a bachelor of arts in sociology, a master of arts in educational leadership, a multiple-subject bilingual teaching credential, an administrative credential, and a doctorate in educational leadership for social justice from Loyola Marymount University Los Angeles.

To learn more about Dr. Isiah's work, visit http://rosaisiah.com, or follow @rosaisiah on Twitter.

Yvette Jackson, EdD, winner of the 2019 GlobalMindEd Inclusive Leader Award, is adjunct professor at Teachers College, Columbia University, in New York and senior scholar for the National Urban Alliance for Effective Education. Dr. Jackson's passion is assisting educators in cultivating their confidence and competence to unlock the giftedness in all students. She is driven to provide and promote pedagogy that enables students who are disenfranchised and marginalized to demonstrate their strengths and innate intellectual potential. Dr. Jackson's approach, called Pedagogy of Confidence, helps educators believe in and value these students and optimize student success, which, for Dr. Jackson, is the basis of equity consciousness.

Dr. Jackson is a former teacher and has served New York City Public Schools as director of gifted programs and executive director of instruction and professional development. She continues to work with school districts to customize and systemically deliver the collegial, strengths-based High Operational Practices of the Pedagogy of Confidence that integrate culture, language, and cognition to engage and elicit the innate potential of all students for self-actualization and contributions to our world. Dr. Jackson has been a visiting lecturer at Harvard University's Urban Superintendents Program, the Stanford Center for Opportunity Policy in Education at Stanford University, the Feuerstein Institute, and Thinking Schools International. In 2012, the Academy of Education Arts and Sciences International honored Dr. Jackson with its Educators' Voice Award for Education Policy/Researcher of the Year. She has applied her research in neuroscience, gifted education, literacy, and the cognitive mediation theory of the eminent cognitive psychologist Dr. Reuven Feuerstein to develop integrated processes that engage and elicit high intellectual performances from students who are underachieving. This work is the basis for her award-winning book, *The Pedagogy of Confidence: Inspiring High Intellectual Performance in Urban Schools*. Dr. Jackson also coauthored *Aim High, Achieve More: How to Transform Urban Schools Through Fearless Leadership* and *Unlocking Student Potential: How Do I Identify and Activate Student Strengths?* with Veronica McDermott, and *Mindfulness Practices: Cultivating Heart Centered Communities Where Students Focus and Flourish* with Christine Mason and Michele M. Rivers Murphy.

Dr. Jackson received a bachelor of arts from Queens College, City University of New York with a double major in French and education, and a master's degree in curriculum design, master of education, and doctor of education in educational administration, all from Teachers College, Columbia University.

Anthony Muhammad, PhD, is a much sought-after educational consultant. A practitioner for nearly twenty years, he has served as a middle school teacher, assistant principal, and principal and as a high school principal. His Transforming School Culture framework explores the root causes of staff resistance to change.

Dr. Muhammad's tenure as a practitioner has earned him several awards as both a teacher and a principal. His most notable accomplishment came as principal of Levey Middle School in Southfield, Michigan, a National School of Excellence, where student proficiency on state assessments more than doubled in five years. Dr. Muhammad and the staff at Levey used the Professional Learning Communities (PLCs) at Work® process for school improvement, and the school has been recognized in several videos and articles as a Model PLC.

As a researcher, Dr. Muhammad has published articles in several publications in both the United States and Canada. He is author of *Transforming School Culture: How to Overcome Staff Division*; *The Will to Lead, the Skill to Teach: Transforming Schools at Every Level*; and *Overcoming the Achievement Gap Trap: Liberating Mindsets to Effect Change* and a contributor to *The Collaborative Administrator*.

To learn more about Dr. Muhammad's work, visit New Frontier 21 (www.newfrontier21.com), or follow @newfrontier21 on Twitter.

Douglas Reeves, PhD, is the author of more than forty books and many articles about leadership and organizational effectiveness. He was named the Brock International Laureate for his contributions to education and received the Contribution to the Field Award from the National Staff Development Council (now Learning Forward). Dr. Reeves was twice named to the Harvard University Distinguished Authors Series. He has addressed audiences in all fifty U.S. states and more than forty countries, sharing his research and supporting effective leadership at the local, state, and national levels. He is founder of Finish the Dissertation, a free and noncommercial service for doctoral students, and the Zambian Leadership and Learning Institute. He is the founding editor and copublisher of *The SNAFU Review*, a collection of essays, poetry, and art by disabled veterans. Dr. Reeves lives in downtown Boston.

To learn more about the work of Dr. Reeves, visit Creative Leadership Solutions at https://creativeleadership.net, or follow @DouglasReeves on Twitter.

Kenneth C. Williams shares his experience and expertise as a nationally recognized trainer, speaker, coach, and consultant in leadership and school culture. A practitioner for nearly two decades, Williams led the improvement efforts at two schools by leveraging the Professional Learning Communities (PLCs) at Work process. Skilled in joining the *why* of the work to the *how* of the work, Williams is known for his powerful and engaging combinations of "heart, humor, and hammer." He is an expert at helping schools build capacity in the collective commitments required of *learning for all* cultures.

Skilled in developing productive, student-focused learning environments, Williams is former principal of the Learning Academy at E. J. Swint in Jonesboro, Georgia, and Damascus Elementary School in Damascus, Maryland. His firsthand experience with transforming challenged schools translates into action-oriented presentations that inspire hope, create a clear vision, and offer practical strategies to those overwhelmed by challenges.

His leadership was crucial to creating a successful professional learning community at Damascus, a challenged school that needed a new direction. The results of his efforts can be seen across all grade levels. Over a two-year period, the school's state standardized test scores revealed a significant increase in the percentage of students performing at proficient and advanced levels. The process of building a PLC at E. J. Swint continues thanks to Williams's work in laying a solid foundation in this underserved community.

Williams earned a bachelor of arts from Morehouse College and a master of science from the University of Bridgeport. He is the author of *Starting a Movement: Building Culture From the Inside Out in Professional Learning Communities* and *Creating Physical and Emotional Security in Schools* and a contributor to *The Collaborative Administrator*.

To learn more about Williams's work, visit Unfold the Soul (www.unfold thesoul.com), or follow him @unfoldthesoul on Twitter.

To book Washington Collado, Sharroky Hollie, Rosa Isiah, Yvette Jackson, Anthony Muhammad, Douglas Reeves, or Kenneth C. Williams for professional development, contact pd@SolutionTree.com.

INTRODUCTION

How to Get the Most Out of This Book

Let's be blunt: most people are afraid to talk about race. In a study published in the *Journal of Experimental Psychology*, Boston University (2020) researchers present data that reveal most adults in the United States, no matter their race or parental status, have profoundly inaccurate ideas about when to talk about race with children, with study participants citing fear of inflicting their own racial stereotypes on children as reason enough to avoid the subject. In education, the extremes of this apprehension regarding conversations about race range from workshop vendors that alienate teachers and divide faculties on the one hand to complete silence on the other. There must be a better way to have this discussion.

Beyond Conversations About Race invites students, teachers, administrators, and community members into respectful dialogue on some of the most challenging issues facing educators in the 21st century. Although the references at the end of this book provide empirical support for our claims about racism, some of the writers of this volume have experienced racism firsthand, and others have observed it. Our expertise is not in the academic study of racism but in our lived experiences and, most important, our work with tens of thousands of educators, leaders, students, and community members. In the chapters ahead, you will find scenarios that vary by age and grade level. While we understand these discussions can be challenging, we argue that talk about race and the impact of racism is much better held in the thorough and caring environment of the classroom than from the chaotic, unfiltered, and sometimes badly informed sources that students will otherwise encounter. They will hear about race, violence, and prejudice no matter our efforts to protect them from difficult realties. In summer 2020, we watched one rising ninth grader dissolve into tears as she heard about the murder of George Floyd for the first time, four weeks after the event. Her tears turned to a hot blaze of anger when she asked her mother, "Why didn't you tell me?" Her parents wanted only the best for her and her siblings—all polite, precocious, and happy. Why mess up summer 2020 with discussions of violent death, screaming protestors, and connections these might have to our own schools and neighborhoods, her parents (and many others) reasoned? You will find the answer to that question in the following chapters, as we seek to guide students, teachers, and parents through the difficult terrain of talking about race.

We will learn, for example, that all of us have biases, including a leading researcher who, as a Stanford professor, eloquently admits not only her own biases but also those of her elementary school child. We will learn that many things, from bus rides to classroom discussions to school assemblies, are not always what they seem. Our goal is not to have the reader agree with us, save for the general agreement that truth is better than illusion and that critical thinking requires not personal criticism but the thoughtful ability to test claims against evidence. The neurologist Alison Gopnik (2016) reminds us that there are scientists lurking in the playpen and stroller, so we need not protect them from the gap between fantasy and reality. Rather, we can, in a loving and age-appropriate way, help them to understand the world around them.

Some readers may worry that elementary school students are too young to have meaningful conversations about race or, more broadly, that race is a political issue, and that politics doesn't belong in school. But the *Economist* disagrees, arguing that it is vital for open and honest discussions to occur in schools and throughout society. Why? In its clarion call for open discussion, it notes:

> A third of black boys born in 2001 will probably spend time locked up, compared with one in 17 white boys. In 1968 black households earned around 60% as much as white households, and owned assets that were less than 10% of those of a typical white family. They still do. ("The New Ideology of Race and What Is Wrong With It," 2020)

If we do not learn together with open minds and hearts, then these realities will remain the same for our children and grandchildren, a prospect we find unacceptable as educators, parents, and citizens. It is essential that educators, parents, and community leaders see the challenges of discussing race not as a "Black issue" but rather as an issue that transcends every racial and geographic boundary. In our work, we have learned how misunderstandings and stereotypes affect all of us, whether the discussion centers on the experiences of Black people in the United States, South Asian populations, or indigenous peoples around the world, to name just a few. Indeed, there are echoes of stereotypes and demeaning characterizations, intentional or not, that we recall being directed toward Jews, Catholics, Irish, Slavs, Poles, and a host of other groups who, at one time or another in our history, were subjected to slurs, "jokes," and discrimination. Our effort in these pages is not to solve the long-standing challenge of dominant groups suppressing others but rather to create an environment in which conversations, however difficult, move from talk to action.

The book is divided into three parts. Part 1 prepares readers for challenging conversations. We consider why talking about race is so difficult for some and how to use sample scenarios as an educational tool. Many parents and teachers use this device with small children, asking, "What if?" to help children learn safety, kindness, and other life skills. Older students and adults use scenarios in order to consider a variety of settings that, at first, are not immediately apparent. While we cannot envision every conceivable scenario, it is a helpful tool—intellectually and emotionally—to engage in experiences when the stakes are low and we can change our minds and ask for greater details. While real life may be the best teacher, we know from our experiences at every level of schooling that we can better prepare students for the experiences of real life through practice in a physically and emotionally safe environment. That is the fundamental purpose of using scenarios as an educational tool.

We then consider how to create a safe space for conversation, tolerating divergent viewpoints, encouraging questions, and making it safe for students and adults to admit that they don't always have the right answer. Indeed, sometimes these scenarios reveal that there is no single right answer. It is this safe conversational space into which we also invite parents and community members. We are veterans of benumbing debates over the years about everything from the teaching of reading to sex, mathematics, and evolution. If we don't get it right, those discussions will be cakewalks compared to mishandled discussions about race, and we intend to get it right. The stakes for our children and grandchildren could not be higher. We conclude part 1 with how faculty and staff members can set an example with civil discourse. Having devoted a good deal of our lives to professional learning for teachers and school leaders around the globe, we find that sometimes leaders engage in the illusion of consensus among staff. We know this is an illusion because without exception, when leaders tell us that they have buy-in from every staff member, then only one of two things is true. Either the real arguments are happening in the parking lot well out of earshot of the leader, or second, the leaders are not really engaging in any sort of rigorous and challenging discussions. Talking about race is rigorous and challenging, and if we expect the students to get it right, then the adults must set an example.

Part 2 provides readers with a variety of scenarios and discussion questions. In middle and high schools, we encourage you to use this book as a supplementary text, allowing students to grapple with the scenarios and participate in choosing the ones that will best lead to a thoughtful classroom discussion. For elementary students, we defer to teachers on how to best convey the information, perhaps reading the scenarios and being attentive to student reactions. We understand that some faculty and parents may think that the topics are too sophisticated or perhaps even too frightening for young ears. We respect your wisdom and judgment on this point but hope that you will also consider ours: students know more, have seen more, experience more, and certainly hear more than the adults in their lives think.

In part 3, we guide the reader from discussion to action. We have been lucky enough to watch elementary students not only grieve about pollution but also get their hands dirty cleaning up their neighborhoods and telling public officials about their experience. We have watched middle and high school students advocate for the homeless, for those in foster care, and for racial justice. None of them need an adult's prompting to tell them what to believe or how to act, only directions to the halls of government where they could make their cases more eloquently than a bevy of lobbyists. Change is difficult, and thus we help readers consider not only the history of successful change efforts but also how change agents have faced disappointment and loss. The history of race in the United States (and other countries), like the history of the United States itself, is not a happily ever after story. But neither is it a story doomed to failure. We can, as a country and as elders, get better, and we believe that, as in times of old, the little children shall lead. We close the book with a call to fulfill our responsibilities as students, teachers, and citizens. We are committed to it.

Part 1

Getting Ready for Challenging Conversations

As we review more than four centuries of enslavement, unequal treatment, and the real presence of racist structures, policies, and practices in schools and elsewhere in society, we could at least agree that a discussion is in order. After yet another televised murder of a prostrate Black man, George Floyd, at the hands of police officers, surely, we could agree that this is something we must talk about together. After honoring the command of the U.S. Supreme Court in its 1954 decision of *Brown v. Board of Education of Topeka* that we desegregate schools with all deliberate speed, we could at least have a discussion of why many ignored that unanimous decision. Discussion, after all, is a low bar, and this book will make the case not merely for challenging discussion but for action, from the classroom to the boardroom, statehouse, and halls of Congress. But it all starts with a discussion, or at least it should.

The definition of *racism* is evolving, as dictionary editors are coming to grips with the expanding application of the term. For example, in June 2020, *Merriam-Webster* announced that it would change the definition to include a section on the systemic nature of racism (Hauser, 2020). That section is reflected in its online edition's entry for *racism*:

1. a belief that race is a fundamental determinant of human traits and capacities and that racial differences produce an inherent superiority of a particular race

2. a) the systemic oppression of a racial
   group to the social, economic, and
   political advantage of another, b) a
   political or social system founded on
   racism and designed to execute its
   principles ("Racism," n.d.)

The challenge of this updated definition of *racism* is that it does not absolve those individual participants in a racist system who are not themselves prejudiced. We find this to be the greatest barrier to conversations about race, because when someone claims, "I'm not a racist," the implication can be there is no further discussion, because to continue the conversation would incorrectly accuse the innocent of racism. But this book is not about guilt or innocence. Rather, as the definition of *racism* suggests, it is about our collective involvement—sometimes beneficial, sometimes not—in an economic and educational system that has disadvantaged people of color.

In 2020, political activist and businessman Ward Connerly (2020) expressed on the influential opinion page of the *Wall Street Journal*, "Some say that America needs to have a conversation about race. I doubt that's a good idea." The author has been influential in not only changing the Constitution of the State of California but also pursuing a national effort to repeal affirmative action. Connerly (2020) argues that, in view of the passage of the Voting Rights Act and the election of Barack Obama to the presidency, the victory for Black voting power has been won and no further work is necessary. If, however, you have no fear of discussion and in fact embrace it as a matter of urgent national and global priority, read on.

The first five chapters of this book prepare readers for challenging conversations. In chapter 1, we reflect on why talking about race and racism is so hard. We encounter the resentment and anger so close to the surface in every discussion about race, and how good intentions and the pretense of heroic actions to improve equity can have unintended consequences. Chapter 2 discusses why discomfort is required for critical conversations about race. Chapter 3 considers why the use of scenarios is so valuable as an educational device. Customarily, we use scenarios with small children when we ask "What if?" questions to help them plan ahead. But when we do the same with adults, the scenarios can hit very close to home, leading to either productive, challenging conversations or conversations that drive resentment and anger beneath the surface. When scenarios are well done, they are realistic and provoke honest conversations. Chapter 4 considers how we create a safe space for conversation. Amy C. Edmondson's (2019) pioneering work on psychological safety provides the evidentiary foundation for this chapter, and we consider the difficulty of challenging conversations and the necessity to create a safe environment in which to have them. These discussions must happen not only within the school walls but also with parents and community members. Chapter 5 identifies how the culture of classrooms, hallways, and holiday celebrations can build bridges and break down barriers that might otherwise lead to silos of real and perceived segregation.

CHAPTER 1

Why Is Talking About Race So Hard?

Words matter. When Ken Williams asks workshop participants to envision a student with a T-shirt labeling him as *at risk* and asks for a description of the student, the majority respond with what is wrong with the student or the family. We will choose pronouns deliberately here, because the majority of students with this label are boys and young men, and a significant majority of those are Black boys and young men. The list of descriptions of this pitiful child at risk includes poor behavior, inadequate literacy skills, a fractured family life, absent parents, poor verbal and written skills, inability or unwillingness to express himself, special education needs (both diagnosed and undiagnosed), behavioral disorders, cognitive impairment, and so on.

Ken then changes the label on the T-shirt from *at risk* to *underserved* and asks the same participants to describe the same student. Note that there is no new information about the student except the label. Now the vast majority of descriptions have to do with food security, emotional support, counseling, family assistance, and other factors participants associate with the student's service and support needs. In brief, when we think of a student as at risk, we resort to factors that we cannot control and primarily focus on the student and his family's deficiencies. When we think of the same student as underserved, we turn the lens on ourselves and our systems both inside and outside of schools. A simple turn of phrase changed from the student and his family being the problem to the schools and all the adults in the system being the solution. This chapter considers how language infects our beliefs, perceptions, and decision-making processes, and we explore conversations rooted in evidence and logic, the importance of admitting what we do not know, the problematic nature of both racial "tolerance" and heroism as a strategy, and the pursuit of equity. As we begin challenging conversations about race, our respectful request is that readers and those using this book for group discussion become fearless.

Why Does Anything I Say Come Out Wrong?

Charged racial discussions are part of our legacy. Generation X (people born roughly from the early 1960s to the late 1970s) represents the first generation of Americans born after the passage of the Civil Rights Act of 1964 and the Voting Rights Act of 1965. While these rights are more secure now than in the days of post–Civil War Reconstruction in the 1800s and pervasive Jim Crow laws of the 1900s, it would be extremely naive to think that suppression of Black votes doesn't persist. Well into the 21st century, manipulation, suppression, and gerrymandering are not only alive and well but also often legal (Cobb, 2019). Nevertheless, complacency pervades discussions of race and racism, with comments such as the following.

- "We had a Black president who won two elections. How can you say that society is still racist?"

- "There are Black congresspeople, senators, and mayors. How can you say that Black voters are suppressed?"

- "Look, the plain truth is that a lot of the inequities in the Black community are due to not race but behavior, including more out-of-wedlock births, crime, and lower educational levels. Those are decisions made by adults, not something caused by white people."

- "I know Black people who have doctoral degrees, went to Harvard Law School, and lead companies. That just proves if you work hard enough, you can make it."

Ken, who describes himself as an extremely open-minded and pragmatic gentleman, suggests that in conversations like this, the answer is not to get angry but, in his words, to "get naked." That is, we must be vulnerable enough to talk not only about the present but also about the past, so that we can better understand the present. Ken suggests that conversations begin with some ground rules intended to create a space safe enough to take risks with what we say and that makes clear we are going to give one another the benefit of the doubt, or more succinctly, give grace.

The first of these is a resort to evidence and logic. For example, it is quite true that young people have a much lower unemployment rate and higher probability of entering the middle class if they follow two rules: (1) graduate from high school and (2) get married before having children. When we think of people who fail to follow these rules, it is easy to have an image of the unmarried high school dropout who has three children, and in our mind's eye, this young woman is probably Black. However, those statistics about the value of a high school diploma and marriage prior to children apply to all people, including white people (Kristof & WuDunn, 2019). Our projections lead to racial stereotypes, not evidence. Ken notes that there are more young Black men in the criminal justice system than young white men. One hypothesis to explain these data are that Black men are just more predisposed to crime. But the evidence is that access to criminal defense attorneys, along with disparate policing policies and sentencing laws, account for racial disparities (Ghandnoosh, 2018). Everyone wants more good citizens of every ethnic group, but a focus on behavior misses the point that structural inequities lead to differences in crime statistics.

This is the sort of analysis we teach to high school students in their statistics classes. They are taught to look for confounding variables—those that might not be measured but can be very important. For example, there are more learning disabilities among Black toddlers than white children of the same age. Is the color of their skin the causal variable, or is the amount of lead in their drinking water and in the paint in their old homes the culprit? The answer is clear, as the Environmental Protection Agency (n.d.) reports that the lead levels in the blood of Black and Hispanic children are higher than in other races, and blood lead levels are strongly associated with learning disabilities. So, we can lecture parents about their child-rearing skills all we want, but if we abandon them to a toxic environment, we fail to address the root cause of the problem.

Ken explains in workshops that every conversation has a context. Some of that context is from contemporary factors affecting racial disparities.

We must analyze our response to student challenges, he suggests, as a coach would analyze an athlete's performance. In the school setting, coaches accept students with a wide variety of backgrounds and physical abilities. When they miss a shot in basketball, coaches help them on fundamental skills, broken down into the smallest increments. Ken uses the example of left-handed dribbling to illustrate how precise great coaching, feedback, and practice can be. There might be more than one hundred discrete skills for a successful basketball player, including not only individual skills but also teamwork, full-court vision, time awareness, and so on. But a great coach addresses these skills one by one. Moreover, coaches focus on factors they can control. Ken has never heard a coach provide advice that says, "Go home and grow six inches." And when teams play the championship game, the officials never say, "You might have won the game, but we are going to subtract twenty points because of the mistakes you made three months ago in practice." Think for a moment about the difference between what the same students with the same abilities and backgrounds receive from a basketball coach compared to what they receive in many classrooms. On the basketball court, they learn five-step conditional defenses. In the classroom, students may regard two-step equations as too difficult. On the basketball court, the results of a mistake in practice are feedback and improvement. In the classroom, the result of a mistake is practice, which is often done as homework with no coaching at all, and a failing grade for not doing the practice well. Moreover, that failure in practice will haunt the student months afterward, as teachers use the average of all work during the semester to calculate the final grade. Music teachers also give students effective practice and feedback, leading a group of young people from painful cacophony to musical gems in a matter of months. Watch the next student concert you attend, and see how many parents and faculty members refuse to clap because, after all, those students made a lot of mistakes in practice three months before.

In sum, we must have conversations rooted in evidence and logic. The next time you hear or want to generalize any group, including Asian, Black, white, Hispanic, or indigenous, challenge that generalization not just as racism but as wrong regarding evidence and logic. We need not wait for federally funded studies to provide the evidence. In your own school, you can conduct the perfect experiment observing students who are successful in one area and failing in another. This experiment is perfect because the people being studied are similar—similar parents, DNA, nutrition, housing, background, and so on. The difference in performance is neither the students nor their parents but rather the differences that happen at school. In our conversations, we must therefore focus not only on the effects of racial disparities but also on the causes.

Why Is Everything About Race?

"Be careful," a board member told Doug Reeves. "She's going to play the race card." Doug must have appeared confused because he received a further clarification. "You know, with her, everything is about race." Doug responded not in anger but with curiosity. The statement "Please say more about that" neither agrees with the claim that everything is about race nor dismisses it but rather asks for elaboration. While our impulse may be to say, "Well, as a matter of fact, it really *is* about race," Ken counsels a different approach. He suggests giving participants the benefit of the doubt in discussions about race. He aspires to get through these conversations civilly and productively, because if a conversation is shut down early, we may never have the opportunity to get to a meaningful depth. We must therefore honor vulnerability and transparency, including when colleagues say, "I just don't know what you want!" When the reply is, "I would like to be treated with respect and decency," the rejoinder is almost always, "But I do treat you that way! I say 'sir' and 'please' and 'thank you,' and I always invite you to participate in staff meeting discussions." Here, there is a crossroads, with one path leading to exasperation, exhaustion, and futility, and the other path leading to learning. Conversations about race must be learning opportunities. For example, in response to a claim that the principal is treating staff with civility and respect, a colleague might say, "I know that you mean well, but sometimes when you ask me for my opinion in a staff meeting, it's not clear whether you are asking my views as a professional educator or my views as a Black person whose view you want to represent the entire race."

Another important ingredient of conversation is a pause lasting not just a few seconds but a minute or more. While every teacher knows in theory about wait time, we hardly ever see that practiced in adult conversations, staff meetings, or collaborative team meetings as professionals.

Stakeholders expect teachers to have the answers and expertise in our fields, but none of us is an expert in how others view race and racism. The best facilitators on this subject have many more questions than answers. Questions that result in silence lay bare our awkwardness and uncertainty, and silence allows us to first consider the assumptions behind the statements we are about to make and the answers we are about to offer.

Ken candidly acknowledges that, despite his lifetime as a Black man and the predominantly white environment in which he lives, he does not have all the answers. That's because being Black or living in a predominantly white area doesn't give all the answers. Our impulse as educators, he explains, is to avoid being wrong, but not wanting to be wrong implies that there are clearly right answers. The answers for racial dilemmas are not going to appear on a test like multiple-choice questions. Learning is about growing, and that requires doubt, uncertainty, and admitting what we do not know. In any complex endeavor, admitting what we don't know is not a sign of weakness or moral frailty but just an admission. If we were teaching a trigonometry class and a student appeared confused about cosines and tangents, we would not assume this misunderstanding was due to racism or some deeply embedded flaw. Rather, both teacher and student would accept that trigonometry is difficult, and to understand it requires work.

We therefore ask you to consider your toughest subject in school, the one that seemed most confusing, frustrating, and seemingly impervious to understanding, in a class you could not drop because you needed it for college. It might have been trigonometry, language arts, or chemistry. Now think about how you responded to that frustration. None of you said, "I think I can knock this out with a three-hour workshop" or "I can just listen to an inspirational speech about calculus." Perhaps you asked for help, participated in a study group, or just read more and worked harder with a trusted study partner who knew a bit more about the subject than you did. Our question is this: For the most important conversations of our time, are you willing to give them at least as much attention as you gave to that class?

Ken had an experience in Canada that helped Doug consider the question of "Why is everything about race?" The entire audience consisted of

First Nations people. Ken's presentation on professional learning communities, supported with abundant evidence and compelling examples, fell flat. Audience members told him bluntly that he lacked perspective, knew nothing about First Nations students and schools, and was just one more American trying to tell them what to do without having invested any energy into learning about them. So Ken stopped, listened, and learned. He admitted his lack of experience and background. He endured silence and exasperation. He asked the fundamental questions, "Why don't I know more about First Nations people? How did I achieve distinction in my profession, write public books, and give keynotes to thousands of people without filling this huge gap in my education?" The only way to address these questions is to accept them as valid challenges that impel us to learn more. No matter how well read, experienced, and expert we may be, great educators are always learners, and the opportunity to learn from others, in this case First Nations elders, is one to be prized. Ken ultimately found common ground among the cultures, including the essential nature of collaboration, exploration, empathy, and a collective need to learn. But it was still a very rough day personally and professionally. None of us want to appear stupid. None of us want to be without answers. Yet when it comes to conversations about race, the first step is admitting what we do not know. Just as it is possible to write a doctoral dissertation about educational leadership and never experience the challenges of being a leader, even the most serious study of racism does not allow us to enter into the diverse lived experiences of people of color. Thus, the first step in dialogue is not sharing our wisdom but listening to others.

What's Wrong With Racial Tolerance?

Tolerance is a pretty low bar. Think of the things we tolerate, like asparagus, curfews, rules, taxes, or parking tickets. It would be difficult to think of a more insulting way to begin a conversation about race than to make tolerance the goal. Most of us do not seek to understand taxes; we just tolerate them. While we find parking tickets irritating, we learn to either avoid them or pay and then forget about them. And we simply avoid some things we especially loathe, like asparagus. Now tell us again that racial tolerance is our objective.

The opposite of tolerance is intolerance, and while this book's goal is reasoned discourse and action, there are surely boundaries. There are times when people of good conscience require intolerance. Ken recalls hoping and praying to get into a gifted class in second grade, and his exclusion wounded him deeply. Ken does not recall his scores on the admissions tests for the gifted program, or if there even was a test. But the fact is that many Black children are underrepresented in gifted, talented, and advanced programs at every level (Card & Giuliano, 2016). Ken vowed to be intolerant of labels and programs that relied on such systematic exclusion. Similarly, we can be tolerant of different perspectives on teaching, but we must be intolerant when differences in teaching lead to systemic inequities. A clear example in the era of COVID-19 and schools attempting to teach students remotely is that some students fail not through lack of intelligence, ambition, or desire but through lack of access to the technology, space, and individual attention that online learning requires. Many schools and educational systems have covered up these disparities through pass-fail grading (Schneider, 2020), but this leads to complacency—the illusion of success without having to confront the challenges.

When we fail to address the disparities in student learning honestly, it is no different from the party host who glibly says, "Well, I invited all my Black friends to the party, and they just didn't attend. Their loss." While tolerance of different ideas may be a virtue, tolerance of toxic policies and practices is a vice. This is a critical distinction in conversations about race and racism. Consider the statement, "Well, I give all my students equal opportunity and lots of support, and their success in my classroom shows that there are zero inequities." This is admirable but insufficient. We can learn much from this teacher's practices that result in zero inequities, but we must home in on the first-person pronouns of *I* and *my*. They clearly signify that equity depends on individual goodwill rather than comprehensive policies and practices. When other classes down the hall persevere in practices and policies that result in inequities, personal rectitude is no substitute for essential intolerance.

Are You Calling Me a Bigot?

Raised in the town that gave birth to the case *Brown v. Board of Education of Topeka*, Doug saw racial inequities firsthand. He also saw people of goodwill grapple with those inequities and was raised by a mother who volunteered to teach Black children to read before they reached elementary school and a father who provided free legal services to laborers on Saturday mornings. In school, Doug debated with and against Black students. In the military, more than a third of the men in his unit were Black, and his 4:30 a.m. to 9:30 p.m. days there included not just command responsibilities but teaching, supporting, coaching, and otherwise helping his colleagues who needed him most. When he won the Brock International Prize that carried a hefty cash payment, he spent that money and much more on building a school in Zambia and helped other white donors do the same. He did everything to establish his racial justice bona fides except add, "And by the way, I have Black friends and neighbors!" These examples are where many discussions about race and racism go off the rails.

The title of Robin DiAngelo's (2018) book *White Fragility* gets at the heart of the issue. While we dissent from the implication that the cure for racism is workshops and speeches, we embrace the notion that essential discussions that occur for years and generations, not just in workshops, depend on an authentic willingness to observe what is missing. However well-intentioned Doug and his similarly minded peers might have been, there is a persistent hero complex in which white people need to save Black people that is distinctly uncomfortable in retrospect.

Many education programs intended to save underperforming students, the majority of whom were not white or did not speak English at home, but if these programs really worked, we wouldn't see the persistent disparities in achievement in 2020 that endure about half a century after the War on Poverty and almost seventy years after the *Brown* decision. The picture of education in movies does not help. From *The Freedom Writers Diary* and *Stand and Deliver* to the 1967 Sidney Poitier film *To Sir, With Love*, teachers are the heroes, overcoming great personal, societal, and administrative obstacles to help their students. However inspiring or saccharine these films may be, they all suffer from a fundamental flaw: heroism is not a strategy. In fact, by their very nature, heroes are exceptional.

The single hero in the building does not defeat the inequities that pervade the school and system, and the fictional activities of these teachers, however wonderful they may be, continue to be worthy of notice precisely because they are not replicable. The audience's focus on the exceptional teacher too often blinds them to the real story: all the unnamed teachers and administrators who started their careers as heroes but gave up the fight.

Ken often notes that nobody became an educator with the purpose of failing students. The vast majority want every student to succeed and grieve when he or she fails. But because schools are stuck in the delivery model of education—educators' job is to deliver instruction, and the job of students is to internalize that instruction and transform it into learning—disproportionate failure rates persist. Therefore, we are responsible not only for our own actions but also for the systems of support for all our students. When we are teaching students to swim, we do not throw them into the deep end in order to learn this skill by risking drowning. Nor do we restrict these students to the shallow end, where they never need to learn to swim because their feet always safely touch the bottom and, importantly, the teacher conveys in a thousand little ways that he or she doesn't expect them to swim anyway.

So no, Doug is not a bigot. But he has been and perhaps still is an enabler of bigotry. This is the essence of challenging conversations. We can take pride in our past, but not focus more on the glow that pride creates than to acknowledge the crystal-clear racism of the present. This is not, we argue, about shedding guilty tears in a workshop, but rather engaging in honest discussions and examining our work and motives on a daily basis.

Will It Be on the Test?

Schools are not designed to achieve our intentions or values. They are perfectly designed for one thing—to achieve results they are capable of. If they achieve equity and excellence for all, that is their design. If they achieve inequity for most and excellence for a few, then no mission statement, list of values, strategic plan, or series of workshops and speeches can change that essential design. If a system prioritizes the job security of administrators and, in some cases, teachers, on test scores, then that is what the system will produce. The following question eclipses any proposal for time devoted to deep examination of the practices and policies that lead to inequities: "Will it help us improve test scores?" The truthful answer is, "Yes, as a matter of fact, the pursuit of equity contributes directly to academic excellence," and there is a substantial body of research that demonstrates that (Reeves, 2020).

Conclusion

Factors that lead to equity and excellence can seem laborious. Professional learning communities, collaborative scoring of student work, multidisciplinary writing, and so on sound good in theory, but when students are taking a mathematics test, how should a teacher use charts about inequities? If a teacher has 190 sophomores who can't add, subtract, or read problems on the test, that's the only immediate focus. This is the logic of the hapless swimming coach who doesn't have time to teach strokes to students who are learning to swim but can only flail in the deep end or become bored and disengaged in the shallow end. Perhaps that's a poor analogy, because when it comes to athletics, we always seem to find ways to get the best out of every student and help him or her achieve remarkable improvements from one week to the next and one practice to the next. Moreover, coaches know that winning is about how we finish the game and the season, not about a series of exercises—and the mistakes that they inevitably entail—that occur during the practices prior to the game. The rest of this book asks why we sometimes fail to apply these coaching lessons to teaching, learning, and leadership.

CHAPTER 2

Why Is Discomfort Required?

Frederick Douglass was once enslaved, only to become the most well-known abolitionist. His most famous quote, "If there is no struggle, there is no progress," is often cited in various education contexts and appears on posters throughout schools across the United States. In that one sentence, Douglass provides a long-standing lesson of life. Any significant, meaningful change is accompanied with a fight, figuratively and sometimes literally. While many know of this quote, few probably know its full context.

In 1857, Douglass gave the speech "West India Emancipation" near Rochester, New York. Much of the speech outlines the history of enslaved West Indians' struggle for freedom from the British, but two paragraphs of his speech foreshadow the human toil and toll of the Civil War. The following shows the quote in its fuller context:

> Let me give you a word of the philosophy of reform. The whole history of the progress of human liberty shows that all concessions yet made to her august claims, have been born of earnest struggle. The conflict has been exciting, agitating, all-absorbing, and for the time being, putting all other tumults to silence. It must do this or it does nothing. *If there is no struggle there is no progress.* Those who profess to favor freedom and yet deprecate agitation, are men who want crops without plowing up the ground; they want rain without thunder and lightning.

They want the ocean without the awful roar
of its many waters. This struggle may be a
moral one, or it may be a physical one, and
it may be both moral and physical, but it
must be a struggle. Power concedes nothing
without a demand. It never did and it never
will. (Douglass, 1857; emphasis added)

As Douglass foreshadowed, the ending of enslavement in the United States would be the penultimate struggle, and the abolition the ultimate progress. His message—no struggle, no progress—is a lesson learned in the context of moving beyond conversations about racism as well. Indeed, Sharroky Hollie would argue, based on his work with hundreds of teachers across the United States, that one of the reasons we remain stagnant around issues of race and racism is because discomfort is not valued as a requirement, thus leaving Douglass's message unheeded. We want to feel good about our work around issues of race and racism. What we learned in the time of Douglass, as well as in the aftermath of summer 2020 with the murder of George Floyd, is that forward movement and action do not "feel good." Discomfort is necessary for any authentic conversation, any radical change. In this chapter, we'll delve deeper into what we mean by *discomfort*, distinguish between discomfort and negative energy, recognize healthy discomfort, learn how to create a support network when experiencing discomfort, and come to celebrate discomfort.

Defining *Discomfort*

Because discomfort is necessary when deeply discussing issues of race and racism, a common understanding is integral. Discomfort is difficult to conceptualize because it can be one of so many things. Sharroky defines *discomfort* as a combination of healthy tension that creates a slight emotional uneasiness, some cognitive dissonance, and an inclination to push through whatever the issue is rather than shutting down. Another way of describing discomfort is stepping out of one's comfort zone. Indeed, many experts on courageous conversations about issues of race and racism, such as Glenn E. Singleton (2015), strongly advise that a facilitator structure and strategize any conversation so that participants will experience discomfort. The purpose of discomfort is to simulate the emotionality that can come with the reality of experiencing racism, particularly for people of color. But the experience of discomfort during a conversation should in no way be mistaken for the actual experience of racism. The key to defining discomfort is to not confuse it with negative energy, as they are not the same.

Separating Discomfort From Negative Energy

Sharroky knows from experience that the main reason many people are afraid of discomfort is that they have confused it with negativity. Even though discomfort may not feel positive in the moment, it should end on a positive note because there will be forward movement, a sense of relief, and a feeling of liberation. When the energy is negative, there is no forward movement. In fact, the conversation or action often stagnates. To help separate discomfort from negative energy, Sharroky offers what he calls *common negative energies* to help people know the difference among them. The rule is when negative energy rears its ugly head, the conversation pauses, and the particular negative energy can be dealt with in the moment. We cannot accept negative energy because it stops the flow of progress. Sharroky defines more than ten examples of negative energy (Hollie, 2017). The following are a few he frequently sees when working with educators around the United States.

- **Most likely:** "Offensitiveness." An overly emotional reaction to concepts or materials that have been presented unemotionally; the reaction may be in the form of an inappropriate question, comment, or, in rare cases, behavior (for example, "Sounds like you are calling me a racist" or "I don't agree with this kind of talk—period; I love all my students").

- **Most annoying:** Hating. Brings unnecessary drama and stress to a situation; a person who always finds something wrong and responds with negative energy (for example, "This room does not have enough light, and they never have snacks for us" or "I have some shopping to do—how much longer will this be?").

- **Most insidious:** Twisting. Taking the facts and twisting them to fit an agenda; this person will tell only half of the story; he or she is an expert decontextualizer (for example, "He said that we should not talk about race—just culture" or "They want the students to be free to do whatever they want").

- **Most harmful:** Myopia. Being unable to see the importance of the bigger picture. The myopic person is stuck in protecting the status quo, justifying his or her action with reasons that usually have nothing to do with the topic (for example, "Why don't they focus on the parents sometimes?" or "We are a high-performing district with a few problems").

- **Most frustrating:** Traditionalism. Traditionalists are believers who are not willing to build. They are simply stuck in the traditional ways of discussing issues of race and racism (for example, "If it ain't broken, why fix it?" or "Our community has not changed much, but our student population has").

Sharroky points out these negative energies to say that they are not examples of discomfort and to remind us that any type of negative energy that enters the conversation is problematic (Hollie, 2017).

Recognizing Healthy Discomfort

Knowing what discomfort is *not* helps with knowing what discomfort *is*. As mentioned, it starts with a healthy tension. A healthy tension is a push and pull between seemingly opposite opinions, perspectives, concepts, or tasks. On the surface, these polar differences present an either-or dynamic, but when we examine while experiencing a healthy discomfort, they become both-and. Common tensions in conversations about issues of race and racism are logic and objectivity versus gut feelings and subjectivity, candidness versus tactfulness, and realism versus idealism. There is power in healthy tension. Another recognition of healthy discomfort is emotional unease, which typically comes with a healthy tension. There is an edge or disquietude in the air that helps foster disruption. However, the line between unease and outright anxiety is very thin, so emotional check-ins are important.

Next is cognitive dissonance, or holding contradictory beliefs or values simultaneously. In other words, a little internal doubt, questioning, and challenging are always good. Being in an echo chamber with your feelings or thoughts will prevent discomfort. Last and most important is liberation. Healthy discomfort comes with an exhilarating feeling of liberation. Sharroky likens it to the experience of feeling lighter because you release whatever burdens you. A big exhale, if you will, and the desire to move forward overtakes you. Unfortunately, because many folks have never felt discomfort authentically or are unwilling to do so, liberation, which is the whole point, is missed and so is the opportunity for change. Again, discomfort is a necessary component, but we must experience healthy discomfort or we defeat its purpose.

Creating a Support Network When Experiencing Discomfort

A support network is essential when engaging in deep, intense, and authentic work around dismantling racism. Technically, a support network is a group of people who can help you achieve a personal or professional goal. Whether it be affinity groups, grade-level collaborators, your happy-hour crew, or your family, having people whom you trust and can really talk to, and who will be honest with you, will make a big difference. In other words, one should not experience discomfort alone. There will be times when you need to talk about what you felt while you were experiencing discomfort.

An advantage of having a support network is that there is power in numbers. More is always better than just one for significant change, meaning forward movement and action are more likely to occur if more people are willing to experience discomfort during conversation and when taking action against racism. Support networks are beneficial to individuals, but collectively they can be a momentum maintainer for the entire learning community. To put it bluntly, who has your back when it comes to discomfort and its associated vulnerabilities?

Celebrating Discomfort

Being willing to authentically converse about issues of race and racism and experience discomfort while doing it takes courage and is hard work. Spending time to celebrate the small steps will keep the energy alive. You should not, however, confuse the celebration of small steps with celebrating the overall accomplishment of any forward movement and action. These steps are like individual miles in a marathon: you save the festivities for the finish line. Keep your celebrations simple, quick, and easy. In most cases, intangible celebrations, such as rounds of applause in the moment, will last longer than tangible ones, like gift cards. These celebrations are really ways of appreciating and honoring one another in racial justice work.

Conclusion

In the spirit of James Baldwin, author Ta-Nehisi Coates (2015) says in his book *Between the World and Me*, "And still you are called to struggle, not because it assures you victory but because it assures you an honorable and sane life" (p. 97). Coates builds on Douglass's historical message, noting that struggle is not just about progress. Discomfort when looked at as a requirement brings honor and sanity to life. Sharroky calls this liberation. Discomfort is required ultimately because racial justice is required—then and now.

CHAPTER 3

Why Scenarios as an Educational Tool?

Educators widely use scenarios, and these scenarios are one of the most helpful strategies for students, faculty, administrators, and policy makers to have challenging and constructive discussions about race. Readers will assess for themselves the degree to which the scenarios in this book, real or plausible, are relevant to events in their schools. We are convinced that the scenarios in the pages that follow meet that test because students suggested many of them in 2020 based on their personal experiences. Others leap from the newscasts. If you find scenarios a useful tool for the classroom, we invite you to create more of them or, if you wish, modify the ones we offer in order for them to be as directly relevant to your classrooms and communities as possible.

How Can We Find Truth Through Fiction?

Very young children learn to separate fiction from truth, or nonfiction, writing. But as they age, they learn that many works of fiction can describe characters, settings, dilemmas, and feelings that strike the reader as absolutely truthful. Poetry can engage our emotions, including describing real events, such as when Walt Whitman memorialized Abraham Lincoln in "O Captain! My Captain!" Similarly, the songs and poetry enslaved people and their descendants sung often did not describe a particular event, but rather a state of being. For example, Bessie Brown's "Song From a Cotton Field" can reach students more than a dry description might now. Consider the lines "All my life, I've been makin' it / All my life, white folks takin' it" (Brown, n.d.). These words illustrate the deep injustices that enslaved people and their descendants who worked as sharecroppers endured. Poetry, songs, stories, and novels can help readers and listeners connect with real-world situations. In the scenarios in part 2 (page 49) of this book, we ask readers to reflect in the same way they might to Brown's lyrics. Why do people feel that way? How do they sing joyfully when the words describe such terrible conditions? A few words can convey complexity, contradiction, emotional dilemmas, and conversational challenges. That is what happens when a teacher uses scenarios skillfully. While the actual story in the scenario may not have happened, the elements of the story are believable and can form the basis for contemplating real events.

Do Scenarios Help Learning?

In fields as diverse as technology, health care, and business, students encounter real-world conditions without the risks associated with, well, being in the real world (Gupta, 2019). Even very young students use scenarios to improve their social and emotional skills (Valdes, 2017). Although educators have long used scenarios as an educational tool, their plausibility limits their value (Cederquist & Golüke, 2016). If the scenarios, inevitably based on past experience, divert too much from future reality, then they lose their educational impact. It is also important to consider that scenarios that seem wildly fanciful, such as 1950s science fiction about journeys to the moon or the ability of humans to do mathematics computations in their heads without a calculator, were eerily prescient. From an educational perspective, the best scenarios allow discussion participants to have confidence that while the characters may be fictional, the situations they describe are real.

How Do We Help Students Construct Scenarios?

Just as one of the best ways to learn to write well is to read widely, students should begin their scenario writing by thinking about the scenarios in literature they have read. Although we encourage teachers to give wide latitude to students in the creation of scenarios, each one typically has four parts: (1) characters, (2) setting, (3) plot, and (4) dilemma. In this book, we base characters on students, teachers, and principals.

For student-created scenarios, however, their characters might include imaginary siblings, parents, classmates, teachers, and people they have heard about on social media or in the news. The settings can vary widely. Think of how students can reflect on traits like courage, cowardice, loyalty, and betrayal, from ancient myths to science fiction. The settings can be widely different, but their relevance to students can be immediate. The plots should usually include some sort of conflict, ranging from a misunderstanding to an emotional wound to an actual fight. We defer to the judgment of teachers to set age-appropriate boundaries for the nature of the conflict in student scenarios, especially those that students will share with the class. For example, gun violence and street fights are part of life for many students, and to omit those plot points would be to distance scenarios from their lives. For younger students, conflict can be real and meaningful but discussions of violence and death overwhelming, so use age-appropriate language when having these conversations. These are matters not for us to prescribe but for teachers and administrators to consider carefully. Dilemmas in a good scenario should leave readers with a question to resolve. There may be multiple solutions or, in many cases, no solution on which the class can agree. The educational value of a scenario is not necessarily through seeking consensus, as many students engage in the illusion of agreement because arguments and disagreement with classmates and teachers seem too emotionally dangerous. One strategy for teachers to consider is the assignment of different ideas to support, so that after alternative solutions to the dilemma are constructed, students do not simply express a preference but invest the time to consider and express different alternatives, even if those alternatives do not represent their personal preference.

The consideration of different points of view is, in our experience, an uncommon feature of many classrooms. The same is true of too many faculty meetings and gatherings of collaborative teams in the context of a professional learning community. When we hear no disagreement, we find that the real arguments take place in the hallway or parking lot or on the playground without thoughtful facilitation in a classroom or team meeting. In the next chapter, we consider how to create a safe space for conversation.

Conclusion

In this chapter, we considered the value of scenarios as educational tools. Realistic scenarios allow students to transcend time and geography to gain a better, if imperfect, understanding of and empathy for the lives of others. Scenarios are more than role playing and can include the sights, sounds, and feelings that might never emerge with mere descriptions of scenes. Educators have long used scenarios as a way to help students understand different settings, and in this book, we use this technique to further authentic conversations.

CHAPTER 4

How Can We Create a Psychologically Safe Space for Conversation?

Learning requires safety. In particular, learning requires an environment of physical, psychological, and emotional safety that allows us to make the mistakes that are an essential part of learning. Every scientist, teacher, leader, and—we hope—student knows that the only way to learn is to make mistakes and get feedback on, understand, and learn from them. We read better when we hear other people tell us what they learned from a passage that we might have missed. We write better when we receive feedback and then edit and rewrite our work. We perform better as athletes, musicians, students, and teachers when it is safe to make mistakes, admit them without humiliation, and learn from them.

Wait a minute! Isn't it true that kids learn to not touch a hot stove by getting burned? Wasn't it the lack of safety that taught them this valuable lesson? Life is full of dangers, after all, and the best way for kids to learn not to climb too high is to fall out of a tree. Kids are too coddled today anyway, right? Besides, experience is the best teacher. Let's step back and consider these ideas. It's quite true that a child might learn that a stove is hot by touching it and getting burned. Perhaps the angry and frightened parent reinforced the message with a spanking, which might leave the child, now sore in two places, with the essential learning that one had better not enter the kitchen. The trip to the emergency room after falling out of the tree might not have resulted in a lesson about the strength of limbs or the potential disorientation that can occur at altitude, but simply a lesson never to climb another tree. While we acknowledge the value of experience, we insist that it is not necessary to hurt other people to learn kindness any more than it is essential to try on bigotry for size in order to become a more fair and decent human being. We really can learn from others—and from our own mistakes—if we are in a safe learning environment. Such an environment is dependent on psychological safety; safety in making conversational mistakes, trying out ideas, and asking questions; and the safety that we must extend to others.

The Importance of Psychological Safety

Harvard professor Amy C. Edmondson (2019) documents how vital mistakes are in learning when considering the example of errors in hospitals. While most of us would prefer to receive treatment from a hospital with a low error rate, Edmondson (2019) suggests that we take a closer look. It's possible that a hospital with a low error rate has such a low degree of psychological safety that staff cover up or underreport errors, and that a hospital with a higher error rate is actually a much safer environment— medically and psychologically—because staff report errors in an honest and timely manner, and the entire organization learns from them. She finds similar results across many different cultures around the world. If the goal is learning, then it must be safe to acknowledge mistakes.

College professors report that the most successful students are not the perfect ones who never erred but rather the students who made plenty of errors and knew about them (Reeves, 2019). The most fragile students in college—those who fall into a puddle of self-condemnation—are those who receive a steady stream of accolades for eighteen years and, in their college years, have to rewrite a subpar paper, recalculate a mathematics problem, or reconsider a thoughtless and insulting comment. Thus, a safe learning environment is not one of constant reassurance that all is wonderful and rosy but rather one in which teachers and peers can listen to a stereotype a student utters and say, "Rodney, what you just said sounded like you were saying that all girls are the same. Please help me understand what you mean" or "Jennifer, it sounds as if you were drawing a conclusion about James based on his haircut. Please help me understand this a little bit better." We best challenge stereotypes, including those at the heart of racism, by helping students to reconsider their own firmly held convictions. This is not a debate but an opportunity, in the words of psychology professor Adam Grant (2021), to *think again*.

Safety in Making Conversational Mistakes

The easiest way to avoid making mistakes in conversations about race is to simply never have them. That occurs when well-intentioned educational leaders and policy makers admonish teachers to keep politics out of education and otherwise avoid any discussions that might be controversial. The reluctance to engage in classroom conversations crosses every discipline, and teachers, administrators, and even students reinforce it in a dozen different ways. In classrooms where some students eagerly raise their hands and, as a consequence, receive an unending stream of praise from the teacher, it is not surprising that silence in the face of uncertainty is the rule. Thus, students who might benefit the most from the teacher's feedback are least likely to receive it because they never raise their hands, are never called on, and never receive feedback that is essential to learning. The result is a downward spiral of learning, in which students whose parents did not read to them when they were infants are less likely to volunteer to read in class. Those who did not do multiplication tables around the family dinner table are less likely to enthusiastically volunteer the answer to mathematics problems than those who had such an advantage. In this model, deprivation leads to reluctance to engage in class, which then leads to less feedback from the teacher, which leads to lower achievement, which leads, over time, to greater deprivation. This is why the decisions for which students take advanced classes are made not in the year those classes are offered but many years earlier. For example, we have worked in an Illinois high school in which admission to advanced mathematics classes was dependent on three years of stellar performance in previous mathematics classes. What led to stellar middle school performance? The identification of students as mathematically gifted in elementary school. The on-ramp and the off-ramp for opportunities in advanced high school classes were established years before students crossed the threshold of the high school. Since *Brown v. Board of Education of Topeka* was first argued on a cold December day in 1952, more than 50 percent of U.S. public school students are African American, yet account for 8.8 percent of Advanced Placement (AP) exam takers and 4.3 percent of exam takers who earn a 3 or higher on at least one exam, the score typically required for college credit (Jaschik, 2019). A gap this large clearly did not begin in high school but has roots in the early years of childhood and, in fact, began long before those students were born. These data help us to have more thoughtful conversations about educational equity. When someone says, "African American students had an equal opportunity to take college classes—they just didn't take it," data suggest otherwise. And we have not even begun to consider the disproportionate allocation of AP and International Baccalaureate (IB) classes to schools whose students are predominantly white. To be clear: this doesn't make white students who take and pass AP tests racists, and it doesn't mean that their teachers, parents, administrators, or board members engage in conscious bias. But it is undeniably true that they benefit from a system that is overwhelmingly biased. If more than 50 percent of lottery players were white, and only 4.3 percent ever won the lottery, every news outlet would demand investigations into corruption.

The study of data is hardly equivalent to lived experience. As we were writing this book, Doug's ninety-seven-year-old mom, Julie, a veteran of tutoring in segregated schools, asked, "What experience do you have to even talk about race?" For better or worse, Doug did not ask her permission to write this book and hope that it meets with her approval. He counts himself fortunate beyond words that his coauthors were willing to have the conversation despite Doug's inexperience.

Safety in Trying Out Ideas

Part of growing as students and continuing our intellectual growth as adults is the ability to try different ideas. Adolescents seek identity, and ask, "Who am I?" Some will respond, "I'm Black," "I'm a doctor," "I'm a feminist," "I'm a Marine," "I'm a teacher," or "I'm an American." Part of resolving the question of identity is experimenting with ideas, some of which feel like comfortable warm clothes one month, and strange, unfamiliar, and deeply uncomfortable the next. In the aftermath of the murder of George Floyd, many white suburbanites who only a few months earlier would have breezily embraced themes such as All Lives Matter and Blue Lives Matter changed dramatically to embrace Black Lives Matter (Stewart, 2020). People who considered reparations for slavery an impossible pipe dream with unworkable administration later listened to arguments and practical policy ideas (Coates, 2014) that, just a few months earlier, were unthinkable. Discussions about the removal of monuments to Confederate States of America generals, an undiscussable subject in many parts of the United States, became the topic of open discussion at the highest levels of military and government office. While the passage of time makes yesterday's ideas that were rebellious and incendiary become today's normal dialogue, it is essential to recall that early discussions of unpopular ideas are distinctly difficult and even dangerous.

As we consider challenging discussions about race, it is important to remember what a *discussion* is. *Merriam-Webster's* first definition is a "consideration of a question in open and usually informal debate" ("Discussion," n.d.). It is therefore impossible to have a discussion unless the participants are willing to entertain ideas in an open debate. Thus, when people engage in nothing more than an echo chamber—the typical round of mutually reinforcing and affirming exchanges of ideas on social media like Twitter (Yiu, 2020)—it can be called talking or typing, but not a discussion. We designed the scenarios presented in part 2 (page 49) of this book to allow students and faculty to conduct real discussions with respectful exchange of ideas. We understand that the First Amendment of the Constitution does not provide unlimited protection of speech, including threats of violence or yelling "fire" in a crowded theater, as the Supreme Court ruled in *Schenck v. United States* (1919). But in summer 2020, we observed discussions in which some of the scenarios you'll encounter in part 2 appeared to be undiscussable. When, for example, a teacher or administrator says, "I couldn't even consider an assembly that honors police officers" or "The last hours of Mr. Floyd's life are too violent to portray on a school stage," it doesn't prevent vigorous debate. Rather, these intransigent declarations move debate from the safe classroom environment to the less safe environment of the parking lots and streets where discussions, which educators and leaders can't moderate, will surely take place. The essential conditions of a safe conversation are mutual respect and mutual purpose (Flemming, 2019). Many protests involve traditional call and response—"What do we want? *Justice!* When do we want it? *Now!*"—but we have never heard someone stop and say, "Marcus, do you have a different point of view you would like to share with the group?"

There is enormous value in the expression and testing of divergent ideas. Indeed, the contention of alternatives is at the heart of creativity (Reeves & Reeves, 2017), and innovative ideas are essential to make progress in racial justice. Because the social consequences of disagreement and dissent can be significant for many students, we have found that creating a safe space for trying out new ideas sometimes requires assigning roles to students so they can separate the expression of an unfamiliar idea with their personal viewpoints. Following are some examples that will help students consider ideas, learn something new, and deepen their insights.

The teacher first poses a question and then randomly divides the class into two groups: *yes* and *no*. Then the teacher poses one of the following questions and gives students a short period of time—perhaps twenty minutes—to find resources and develop arguments to support their position. Then students express their views in three-to-five-minute presentations, listen to the other side, and consider if they have changed their minds. You can modify the following questions to more appropriately fit the grade level and curriculum, so these are simply ideas to generate the discussion questions that will be most helpful for your students.

- Was Abraham Lincoln a racist?
- Was slavery the cause of the Civil War?
- Did the U.S. Constitution accept slavery?
- Did the United States pay reparations to people from Native Nations tribes whose land was confiscated?
- Do African American defendants in criminal cases receive the same treatment as white defendants facing comparable charges?
- Do African American families have as equal access to purchase homes and rent apartments as white Americans?
- Should every ethnic group in our school have its own school-recognized club?
- Will a focus on Black Lives Matter reduce our focus on the #MeToo movement?

Our fundamental point is that classrooms must be safe places to explore ideas. Students often express viewpoints in lockstep with their parents, influential peers, teachers, or social media. The risk of unpopularity and disapproval is greater than the reward of considering new ideas. That makes it all the more important for educators and leaders to create discussion and debate as an integral part of the educational process.

Safety in Asking Questions

Children can ask embarrassing but curious questions, such as "Why is that woman in a wheelchair?" "Why is that man scrunching up his face?" "Why is that girl's skin so dark?" "Why does that boy smell so bad?" While the tendency of many adults is to expunge the question with a quick start and a "Hush!" we would be wise to consider the question behind these questions. What children really want to know is, "Why are other people so different from me?" While parents forge their own course in how to teach their children about diversity, we believe that educators have a primary responsibility to address these fundamental questions candidly and honestly, with respect for the questioner and the question. When students cannot discuss differences and we suppress questions about these differences, then learning about diversity is impossible. It is not enough to tolerate questions; we must *welcome* them. Indeed, we must help students to generate them. If we fail to do this, then we are leaving students to the unfiltered and often destructive hypotheses of the internet. For example, as author David M. Goldenberg (2003) writes, generations of children were taught that dark skin was the result of the curse of Ham, in which the son of Noah was exiled to Africa and ordered to serve his other, presumably white, brothers and their descendants of slavery. Although other pseudoscientists took a different point of view, arguing that melanin made people of African descent superior to all other races (Ortiz de Montellano, 1993), this is equally odious from an educational standpoint. Our students need, from a very early age, to learn to listen to claims and then ask, "Is that true?" When students and adults stop asking these questions and stop testing claims—on the internet, from friends and family, and in the classroom—against evidence, then their intellectual growth stops. Teachers arrive at a crossroads in their career when they must choose between the path of simply answering questions, the job of the all-knowing expert, to asking questions. The latter course is often uncomfortable, particularly when long pauses follow with students reluctant to express an alternative point of view. But that is the difference between education as a delivery machine and education as a learning environment.

Asking questions in a safe environment is also important for adults. In a conversation with colleagues about differences in the capitalization of the word *Black* to describe African Americans, Stacy Scott exclaimed, "I don't care about the pronouns or what you call me. Just call me alive!" (personal communication, October 1, 2020). He made the point that an overly intellectual focus on pronouns and capitalization trivializes the issue of Black people being murdered. The alternative to questions and discussion is silence and quiet subservience, and that is the opposite of a safe learning environment.

Safety to Others

Students and most adults are better at expecting safety for their own statements than they are at giving assurances of safety to others. We have equipped students to voice their concerns about personal and emotional safety by saying "That makes me uncomfortable" or "That sounds racist" when they encounter threatening words and actions. We also must equip our students to deal with challenging ideas by confidently expressing their own views. Moreover—and this is the most difficult part for learners of any age—we must also help them understand that changing our views is not a sign of weakness. Harvard professor Richard F. Elmore (2011) gathered some of the leading voices in education to explain how they had changed their minds over the years. In *I Used to Think . . . And Now I Think . . .*, the respondents consider how their minds have changed over the years (Elmore, 2011). The title invites an interesting critical-thinking exercise for leadership meetings. We have often posed the question to educational leaders, "What did you know was true ten years ago that, based on further reflection and new evidence, you know is not true today?" We receive astonishingly few responses. If that is true for adults with many years of advanced education, then we can better understand how difficult it is for students and their teachers to change their minds. When learning to walk and ride a bicycle, they are willing to make mistakes, change their behavior, and improve. But many ideas, including those about race, can become ingrained very early, and changing those ideas and the behaviors associated with them can be exceptionally challenging. When people do change not only their espoused attitudes and beliefs but also their behaviors, that is clear evidence of learning and deserves to be celebrated. If we are to create a safe learning environment, then we must take care not merely to honor well-spoken prior convictions but also to honor those who say, "I haven't thought of it that way before" or "Let me reconsider my position on this." Those words are the hallmarks of great classrooms, staff meetings, and professional learning seminars.

Conclusion

In this chapter, we considered the importance of psychological safety. In order for individual and organizational learning to take place, students, teachers, and leaders must be able to admit mistakes, talk about them, and learn from them. The opportunity to make mistakes, including conversational mistakes, mistaken ideas, and poorly framed questions, is a daily event in schools. Our job as educators is not to create perfect mistake-free students but rather to help students understand the value of mistakes, including their own and those of others. Real discussion, we learned, is not about the transmission of ideas from one person to another but rather about considering and debating alternative points of view. This does not come easily to students who often avoid anything resembling conflict or disagreement with peers. That is precisely why giving safety to others is paramount. We now consider how to engage parents and community members in these challenging discussions.

CHAPTER 5

How Will Faculty and Staff Set the Standard for Challenging Conversations?

A school community is a complex amalgam of people: educators, students, parents, community leaders, and others. Many develop professional and personal relationships, and, as in other casual relationships, we share limited parts of our lives, thoughts, and considerations about race relations in the United States and the community we serve as educators. Many of us have an intrinsic and clear understanding of the unwritten codes of what lines not to cross so as not to offend across racial lines or commit a racially insensitive faux pas. But when we consider the care we take not to offend, we are also left to wonder to what extent that attitude also restricts our ability to relate to one another and truly engage in challenging conversations about race. How does that "respect" restrict our understanding of the people with whom we work, the students we educate, and the communities we serve?

These poignant questions require us to consider the fact that we may work with people who personally perpetuate or suffer the indignities of racism. These experiences may give them a unique perspective as they see the protests and racial tension the United States has been experiencing. Some of these colleagues, on different sides of the conversation, may have heard discussions at home growing up that they would never disclose, but that were instrumental in informing their thinking and conclusions about people whose race or socioeconomic status are different from their own.

All these people, along with their closely kept conversations and ideas, converge in a school building in their roles as teachers, students, administrators, parents, guidance counselors, custodians, clerical personnel, and other stakeholders. They may carefully respect those unwritten conversational boundaries and still mindfully render a judgment, come to a conclusion, or intervene with someone from another race, while others may not be so tactful or fair. We must explore the importance of candor in our discussions about race, the types of exchanges that build trust, opportunities to highlight diversity in a tangible way, and expressions of gratitude.

Candor and Honesty as Building Blocks to Strong Foundations

In the school Washington Collado led, changes in school attendance boundaries led to an increase in the percentage of Black and Latinx students and an increase in students qualifying for free and reduced lunch by almost 30 percent over a few years. Those on the leadership team decided to delve into race relations and other difficult topics, and they committed to study racial justice to help students better deal with the reality that many socioeconomic and racial factors were playing out in their hallways, cafeteria, and classrooms. It wasn't enough to have peace; they wanted to empower their students and equip them with tools to be courageous about their differences—to not just tolerate but accept, understand, and engage.

Washington and his colleagues decided to lead by example and began the training process with a staff exercise that applied the work on challenging conversations (Singleton, 2015). The table was set. They called a faculty meeting to provide the training, and the staff streamed into the media center: some excited; some reluctantly compliant with yet another faculty training; and others, Washington was sure, who felt they could find better things to do with their time. They were in for a surprise! One faculty member, Coach Charles, opened his heart about his experience. His students respected him, and he was among the first people to be willing to serve as a mentor to younger teachers and students alike. It was his turn to speak. He was deliberate and calm, and his voice carried a sense of peace and quiet delivery that was not to be misinterpreted as an attack or a misguided indictment on anyone. He was simply sharing his experience; it was a life's lesson on how this man they had come to respect carried scars and painful experiences that they may never fully understand. They didn't live them; he did. The staff quietly listened and reflected about how they were carrying scars from different experiences that affected them in different ways.

In the same manner, other staff from various racial groups and ethnicities shared their own experiences. This meant that the lens through which they saw the interaction of students of color was enriched not only by their own lived experience but also by the guarded limitations societal conventions imposed that make it difficult for anyone to really understand others' points of view, feelings, and conclusions. Washington concluded that this established the value of facilitating civil discourse, and it was evident that his colleagues had to build a positive and engaging approach to support one another and value others' experiences.

Opportunities to Share: Coffee Conversations

As educators, when we hear *challenging conversations*, many things may come to mind: differing opinions, confrontations, tensions, and other adversarial exchanges. Challenging conversations are an important part of discussing topics that need attention, and oftentimes, participants cannot avoid discomfort. However, to build a trust level within the organization that can withstand the pressure of challenging conversations, we must consider investing time and energy in fostering collaborative exchange among teachers and staff and infusing activities that build interpersonal relations within the school and community. Where there is trust, people respect different ideas, and there's room for learning and growth.

As principal, Washington has always seen the value of *coffee conversations*. Staff can build lasting and trusting relations by simply finding opportunities to talk over coffee and get to know each other's interests along with professional and personal motivations. When we purposely look for the staff to interact as colleagues, without specific operational agendas, and engage in conversations with one another, we build trust because the human element and motivations are better known.

The school year provides perfect opportunities for these types of interactions to occur, during observations of Thanksgiving, Hispanic Heritage Month, Black History Month, Christmas, Hanukkah, Ramadan, Diwali, National Indigenous Peoples Day, and so on. At Washington's school, it became customary to take advantage of every opportunity to celebrate, talk, and entertain coffee conversations. For instance, staff brought food that elevated cultural pride and joy for everyone—teachers and clerical and custodial staff. For the Thanksgiving holiday, the table boasted a turkey but also Italian, Latin, and soul foods, desserts, and nonalcoholic beverages. Having conversation over a meal created a genuine family-like atmosphere.

What the School Hallways Say

As the students and teachers walk to class, what do they see on the bulletin boards, in their classrooms, and on the school's marquee? Schools celebrate what they value, and students and staff see it and sense what the school highlights as important. When departments were asked to create bulletin boards and update them with pertinent and timely information, the staff welcomed the initiative. Teachers were keen to portray diverse information and showed prominent figures who genuinely reflected a variety of Americans who have excelled in different areas. In the school's College Square, a high-traffic area, students saw display banners and logos of the traditional big-name colleges and universities. A group of teachers created a very well-done Historically Black Colleges and Universities (HBCU) board that became the focal point, much to the pride of teachers and students.

To highlight diversity and pride across subject areas, consider showcasing the work of every department by conducting a series of academic fairs, showcases, open mic literary nights, shows, and celebrations to bring the community into the school for events the teachers and students organize themselves. Every event can begin with the appropriate salute to flag and country and recognition of teachers and staff, who usually come out to partake in the festivities. While the bulletin boards are helpful, more substantive conversations and education should also follow so that displays lead to direct improvements in teaching and learning.

Recognition and Gratitude Go a Long Way

Schools with low morale tend to silo sections and isolate work in small cliques that are overly critical without aiming to be constructive. On the other hand, there are those faculty members who become reliable sources of support and guidance, or simply resources to share the many frustrating situations teachers face. How can administrators recognize these teachers or celebrate their valuable camaraderie without embarrassing them or exposing them to unwanted attention? Simple: pick-me-ups. The school understands pick-me-ups to be an expression of gratitude toward a colleague. At the conclusion of every faculty meeting, the staff may use the precious final minutes to simply say "thank you" to one another for simple deeds of kindness or complicated and cumbersome acts of teamwork. The result for the rest of the staff may be a feeling that true collaboration is happening in the organization. It is a simple display of teamwork that showcases the result of a successful, supportive network that entices teachers to support each other.

Conclusion

Communication, communication, communication! There are hundreds of key moments during a school year when it becomes necessary to be frank and truthful, and where colleagues do not misinterpret candor as aggression. That atmosphere must be built on trust. Schools comprise people who experience or perpetrate an amalgam of racist or prejudicial acts. How these experiences shape their views of racism and race-based discussions may affect their judgment as they interact with colleagues and students. Candid yet respectful conversation provides opportunities for faculty and staff to empathize and to relate to one another. An organization's members should also find opportunities to discuss, celebrate, and show gratitude to one another. In turn, these positive exchanges can set the tone so that more challenging conversations may have positive outcomes based on mutual respect, understanding, and compromise.

Part 2

Using Scenarios for Important Conversations

In part 2, we offer scenarios for a range of classes, from elementary school to secondary school, and for discussions among classroom educators in grade-level, department, and leadership teams and among district cabinet officers, board members, parents, and community leaders. Our goal is not unanimity but rather mutual understanding of diverse and divergent points of view. Our experience in presenting these scenarios suggests that the facilitator must be aware of three key factors.

First, although the scenarios are based on realistic situations, many of which we have personally encountered, we have deliberately disguised the names in and locations of these scenarios. Therefore, there is no judgment as to the right or wrong answer about what happened in these cases. Indeed, a key point of the exercise is recognition that right answers can be elusive, and deeper thought on a range of possible solutions may be necessary.

Second, disagreements can be immensely valuable because they suggest gaps or ambiguities in school and district policies. We have seen shouting matches ensue when different leaders and teachers react to the same scenario in dramatically different ways. The impact of these differences is that parents might observe that three different classes or schools have three very different responses to a scenario, and that will inevitably lead to accusations of inconsistency and unfairness. When this happens, leaders and policy makers must decide the extent to which principals and teachers will benefit from policy guidance and consistency.

Third, however challenging these conversations are, we hope that each scenario allows teachers to model for students the deep listening, respectful attention, thoughtful disagreement, and civil discourse that are the heart of great schools and a democratic society.

Chapter 6 addresses the distinction between bias and racism. The evidence is clear that bias is a part of life and that part of teaching our students and colleagues to think critically requires that students and teachers alike identify and acknowledge bias. Whether bias is in a political poll, the claim of an advertiser, or the ways in which we evaluate students, teachers, and leaders, the question is not whether bias is present or absent but rather, What are the causes and impacts of it?

In chapter 7, we consider context. Ken Williams suggested in chapter 1 (page 11) that context must include the present generation along with previous ones, and Sharroky Hollie takes us further back into four centuries of history. The enslavement of Africans began long before the Declaration of Independence proclaimed that "all men are created equal," and the Constitution, whose signees include slave owners, declared unequivocally that some men counted less than others and, in a supreme contradiction, were so valuable as property that they were worthless as human beings.

Chapter 8 considers the issue of responsibility. While we no longer traffic people to slaveholders, we share responsibility for the multigenerational impact of that enslavement. Our youngest primary-school students understand the difference between fault and responsibility, but we have found this concept to be more elusive for adults.

Equity cannot only encompass policy and procedure, as chapter 9 argues. All of us, students and adults, share the responsibility for advocacy. Our duty is not merely an impersonal embrace of an ideal but a very personal duty to one's friends.

Chapter 10 addresses the overwhelmingly difficult and emotionally charged issue of law enforcement and race. Ken is not only a leading voice on equity but also the son of a police officer, and thus offers a unique perspective on a subject that many people find explosive to discuss. We submit that one of the ways to honor the memory of George Floyd, whose murder transfixed a nation and provoked a seismic shift in the acknowledgment of the Black Lives Matter movement, is to have challenging conversations about the role of law enforcement in our society.

In chapter 11, we consider race and racism in school as we address this question: Where are the Black people? The research evidence on how children's understanding of race changes over time, and our collective responsibility for it as teachers and parents, will lead to challenging conversations from different perspectives.

Just as bias is different from racism, we learn in chapter 12 that avoiding racism is not the same as active anti-racism.

CHAPTER 6

Talking About Bias: How Can I Be Biased When I'm Not a Racist?

One of the most challenging subjects to talk about when we consider race and racism is that most people think they are fair. Good people, they reason, do not wish to be unfair to Black or Brown people. In their opinion, their parents and teachers taught them not to be prejudiced, and although they sometimes hear racist phrases in the hallway or in movies or see racist actions on the news, they know that they are personally not racist. They have never used the N-word—at least not in a hurtful way, they think—and they have friends who are from Black and Brown families. In this chapter, we explore what the term *bias* means and how bias affects everyone. Sometimes bias helps us and sometimes it hurts us, but it influences us all.

The Meaning of *Bias*

Many people think that the word *bias* is about prejudice. When we say that someone is biased against a Black or Brown person, for example, we are saying they are making a judgment about that person based on the color of his or her skin. But that doesn't really get to the complete meaning of bias. In fact, bias is any conclusion we draw that depends inappropriately on some information and excludes other, more relevant information. If your school calculates your final grade with extra weight given to a final exam, then that calculation is biased toward the final. If the school weights calculation more heavily toward homework and class participation, then the grade is biased toward those factors. Bias, in other words, is not an accusation against you or anyone else—it's just a fact. It's like gravity—bias is always out there, so it's best if we understand it.

The truth is, anyone can be biased, and almost all of us are. Stanford professor Jennifer L. Eberhardt (2019), who is African American, acknowledged that when she first entered a largely white school, she could not tell the difference in the facial features of her white classmates. They simply all looked alike to her. More tellingly, she revealed that when she took her five-year-old son on a plane, he saw an African American man and asked Eberhardt if the man was going to rob the plane. The kindergarten-aged child had no obvious reason to be biased against a Black man, yet there it was—drawing conclusions based on the stranger's appearance. If Eberhardt and her son can be biased, then we might all want to take a breath and admit that we can be biased as well.

How Bias Helps and Hurts People

Normally we just think of bias as something that hurts people—like racism. But an important part of understanding racial injustice is also understanding how bias helps people. Doug knows that he benefited from parents who read to him at a very young age, and dinnertime discussions helped him develop a good vocabulary. That gave him confidence in school that probably made teachers think that he was capable and intelligent. They were biased in Doug's favor even before they had any evidence to believe that he could be a decent student. Anthony drives a car that might cause some people to assume he is successful, intelligent, and hardworking, even though they have not met him— they just make a biased judgment about Anthony based on his car. But for every person bias helps, there are others it harms. Children arrive in the United States every day who are extremely intelligent, but who don't speak English at home and don't have the vocabulary that Doug or Anthony did as a child, so some people might draw negative conclusions about their intelligence and capability. Teachers do not even ask them to consider advanced classes or gifted and talented programs because, after all, they don't seem ready for them. Similarly, some adults drive cars that are old and in disrepair, don't wear nice clothes, and may not smell very good, so even before other people meet them, they can draw conclusions about the intelligence and capability of those adults. That might influence an employer to not even consider them for a job, an unfair act that hurts not only the adult with the old car but also everyone in the family depending on him or her for food and shelter.

Scenarios About Bias

Now that we know that bias can help and hurt, let's think about three scenarios and how to talk about them. The first involves the simple act of getting to school. Whether you walk, take the bus, ride with a parent, or take public transportation, you might notice some patterns of how people of different races act toward one another. The second scenario is about taking a test in a class when there's more to the story than the teacher may see. Third, we'll consider how some students ask for help and others don't, and how bias might influence this seemingly simple action that is so essential to student success.

Getting to School

Every day, Marie takes the bus to her middle school. She always saves a seat for her friend Sophie, who gets on the bus two stops down from Marie's usual bus stop. One cold morning, a new student Marie didn't recognize boarded. The new girl sat next to Marie, but Marie said, "I'm sorry, this seat is saved for Sophie." The new student said, "There's no saving seats on the bus, and don't tell me what to do!" Then, in a surprisingly friendly voice, the new girl stuck out her hand and said, "I'm Thomasina, but you can call me Tommy." Marie was surprised and a little scared and didn't say anything. When Sophie got on the bus, Marie moved to sit next to Sophie. Tommy yelled, "What's wrong with you? Are you too good to sit next to me?" Marie burst into tears and didn't know what to say. When she finally arrived at school, she was afraid to tell anyone why she was so upset.

> **Discussion question: What advice would you give to Marie, Sophie, and Tommy?**

Taking a Test

Jeff hated algebra. He had never been good at mathematics, but he especially disliked the way that his teacher, Mr. Boomer, seemed to ridicule him whenever he didn't know the answer. "I can see you're a real genius," said Mr. Boomer sarcastically. On this day, Jeff was especially exhausted and upset. He had helped his mom with a double shift at the convenience store the afternoon and night before, so he not only missed class in the afternoon but also was up until past midnight before he even began studying for the algebra test. "It's hopeless," thought Jeff. "Boomer's right; I'm a loser." When the tests were handed out, Jeff grew anxious, then angry. "What's the matter?" asked Mr. Boomer. "If you really wanted any help, you could have come by after school yesterday." Rather than explain that he was working to help his mom, Jeff threw the test on the floor. "To the office!" shouted Mr. Boomer. And with that, Jeff walked out of the classroom and the building, not knowing if he would return. Although the principal had been concerned that almost all the students Mr. Boomer disciplined and failed were African American, the teacher insisted he was in the right. "That kid was out of control!" said Mr. Boomer. "And I've got witnesses! That kid needs to be out of here." Some other teachers backed Mr. Boomer, telling the principal that to allow Jeff back in class would just be playing favorites.

> Discussion questions: What should the principal do? What advice can you offer to Jeff? Should Mr. Boomer give Jeff another chance?

Asking for Help

Charmaine and Patrice were best friends. They had sleepovers almost every weekend and confided in each other about boyfriends. They had pretty good relationships, at least for high school juniors, with their parents. Patrice loved that Charmaine's family accepted her and loved the music when she visited their church, an African Methodist Episcopal church in which Charmaine's parents were leaders. Patrice knew that Charmaine was really smart, as Charmaine would help her with mathematics homework and explain things on the internet that were more difficult for Patrice to understand. But Patrice couldn't understand why Charmaine was failing biology. The teacher, Ms. Porter, was nice enough, and whenever Patrice was having trouble in class, she would always go to Ms. Porter after school and ask for help. "Just keep coming," Ms. Porter assured Patrice, "and you'll do just fine in this class." Patrice confronted Charmaine and asked, "Why don't you come with me? Porter's not a pushover, but she's OK—she'll help you." "I don't need to ask for help," replied Charmaine. "I've got this far on my own, and I don't need her to tell me what to do. Besides, I'm getting As and Bs in every other subject, so I'm doing OK." Patrice was worried. "You just can't flunk, Charmaine. You're smart, and you can get a scholarship and go to college, but if you flunk this class, that's not going to happen." Charmaine coolly replied, "I said I don't need help—not from you, not from Porter, not from anybody at that school." Patrice did not understand why Charmaine was so angry when she was just trying to be a good friend.

> Discussion questions: Why do you think Charmaine doesn't want to ask for help? What should Patrice do? Should Patrice talk with the school counselor?

Conclusion

In this chapter, we explored bias—how individuals and sometimes institutions, like schools, make judgments about people without having the information to draw an accurate conclusion. In these scenarios, we learned how even good intentions, as when Patrice was trying to help Charmaine, can lead to misunderstanding. We also saw how teachers can think that they are offering good help but, despite their offers, sometimes students can't or won't seek help. Bias can hurt, and part of growing in our understanding about race is learning how bias also aids people every day. Finally, it's important to remember that bias is not a character flaw. Admitting that you are biased does not mean that you are a bad person, but it does mean that all of us, students and teachers, probably need a lot more information about a person before making a decision about him or her.

CHAPTER 7

Talking About History: How Does the Shadow of 1619 Affect Us Today?

A ugust 2019 was the four-hundredth anniversary of the arrival of enslaved people on the shores of Jamestown, which would go on to be a part of the United States. More than a century and a half before the Declaration of Independence and the Revolutionary War that secured the country's independence, the nation was built on the forced labor of men, women, and children from Africa and their descendants. The Pulitzer Prize–winning 1619 Project from the *New York Times* (Hannah-Jones, 2019) was a massive undertaking of research, and for many Americans, including history teachers and students, it marked the first serious inquiry into the origin and fundamental role that slavery played in the founding of the nation that ultimately became the United States.

Some critics of the U.S. educational system have pointed out—rightly, in our view—that we do not teach enough history in school, and that a deeper understanding of history informs the context of everything else we study, including literature, science, and mathematics. This deeply rigorous and analytical approach to education is precisely what critics would seem to want. Every time schools and states publish low test scores, the critics clamor for "more rigor" in the classroom. It requires interdisciplinary academic rigor, for example, to understand what the Three-Fifths Compromise in the Constitutional deliberations meant for the political and economic future of the nation. Similarly, a blend of history and literature is required to understand the impact of *Uncle Tom's Cabin*, *The Last of the Mohicans*, and, decades later, *Gone With the Wind* and *The Lone Ranger*. Students must understand the scientific method and mathematical probabilities to understand and challenge

59

pseudoscientific explanations for the racial superiority of whites. There is, therefore, little disagreement about the need for rigorous study of the origins and impact of slavery.

Just kidding! There is great disagreement around teaching about slavery because, as a U.S. senator, Tom Cotton (as cited in Cole, 2020), suggested in summer 2020, the practice was simply a "necessary evil" that, however uncomfortable for enslaved Africans, was just the way it had to be. Moreover, Cotton claimed, teaching students about slavery, as the 1619 Project does, is "a racially divisive, revisionist account of history that denies the noble principles of freedom and equality on which our nation was founded. Not a single cent of federal funding should go to indoctrinate young Americans with this left-wing garbage" (as cited in Cole, 2020).

We hope schools will welcome this debate, because the necessary evil defense pervades history to present day. It was politically expedient in the 20th century to defend the internment of Japanese Americans during World War II; by Chairman Mao, Hitler, and Stalin to defend the deaths of millions of their countrymen; and in the 21st century to defend inhumane prison conditions, inadequate health care, and unsafe housing (Kristof & WuDunn, 2019). When our students hear from a public official, whether in speeches of the previous century or from the previous day's news that "It's all quite unpleasant—just a necessary evil," we want them to be prepared to challenge that contention. Our purpose in this book is not to indoctrinate students or censor history but rather to equip everyone in education to engage in challenging and fully informed conversations.

The Myth of Balance

Imagine that a science teacher, committed to the principle of hearing all sides of every argument, decided that it was important to "teach both sides of the gravity question." After all, Newton's opinion on the subject is only one of several equally valid perspectives. As preposterous as this sounds, pseudoscience has been not only popular but also a prescribed part of the curriculum in schools. These perspectives are not in the backwaters that 21st century hipsters find so easy to ridicule but in the halls of the nation's leading universities. Harvard was only one of many institutions of higher learning that followed a long line of scientific proof to confirm stereotypes with the veneer of science, "proving" the inferiority of not only Africans but also the Irish, Chinese, Slavs, Italians, and any other group for which society needed science to support subjugation (Gould, 1996). If teaching "both sides" of the gravity question sounds preposterous, then consider that in the early 20th century there were vigorous academic debates about eugenics and the building of a superior race—not in Hitler's Germany but in the august halls of U.S. universities. In the last part of the 20th century and into the third decade of the 21st century, there were and are serious debates about racial determinism (Herrnstein & Murray, 1996) and the role that slavery played in our nation's history.

The question educators face is not whether to have challenging conversations but how best to teach students to have them. While we have had class discussions since Socrates cross-examined Plato in the Lyceum, we have also known that Plato's legacy of racism—men of gold, silver, and bronze—is no longer worthy of debate. In the 21st century classroom, we can debate the merits of technology, but it is a waste of time to discuss whether or not technology exists. Teachers are obliged to help students ask questions and formulate vigorous arguments from different perspectives, but they are not required to waste time on either proving the obvious or disproving the odious. In sum, it's a thoughtful use of class time to inquire about why slavery came to be and why it persisted in the United States, and what the lingering effects of enslavement of millions of people are. It is not a useful expenditure of time to ask whether or not slavery was justified.

The Need to Understand and Assess Culture

The very word *culture* is loaded with potential for abuse. The definition seems benign: according to *Merriam-Webster*, it is "the customary beliefs, social forms, and material traits of a racial, religious, or social group" ("Culture," n.d.). But the connotation of the term is laden with implications that range from laudatory to damning. For example, when we refer to a person as *cultured*, the implication is that he or she is refined, well-bred (another loaded term), polite, knowledgeable, and otherwise a welcome member of high society. The same term can have the opposite implication, such as a *culture of abuse* or *culture of hate*. Strictly speaking, the residents of Europe and North America who enslaved Africans were *cultured*, not because they were particularly courteous and intelligent but because they enacted the customary beliefs and social norms of their racial, religious, and social groups. Just as it is historically inaccurate and ethically bankrupt to refer to slaveholding Europeans and their descendants as cultured in the positive sense of the word, it is equally wrong to follow, as some educators have, the path of cultural relativism that proclaims that all cultures are equally valid ("Are All Cultures," 1998). Part of the critical thinking that should emerge from an understanding of the history of enslaved peoples is that it is not a culture that is right or wrong; it is the practices that those cultures validate. Cornell professor of Black studies Sandra Greene (as cited in Swift, n.d.) notes that while about twelve million Africans were enslaved and sent to North America, millions more were retained as slaves in Africa. Slavery was no better in Ghana than in the United States, and therefore an essential part of our challenging conversations about race and racism is that we confront and assess evil wherever it happens (Swift, n.d.). Professor Greene and her colleagues help us understand that Black studies and an Afrocentric curriculum are not about uncritical praise of everything African but rather about how every culture must both celebrate its achievements and critically examine its failings. The pervasive nature of enslavement on every continent and throughout history is a vivid reminder to our students, colleagues, and communities that freedom is a rare and precious commodity, and the lives lost and futures slavery shattered formed the foundation not only for the wealth of plantation owners then but also for all of us today.

Scenarios From the Classroom to the Dinner Table

These scenarios are designed for discussion among students and teachers as classroom activities. In addition, students involved in a current affairs club or debate society might find these useful prompts for discussion.

Amistad in the Lunchroom

Jefferson Williams and Jefferson Thomas attended school together since kindergarten. They always insisted on being called by their full first name—never *"Jeff"* or *"Jeffrey,"* but the name they were given. Although they had occasional times of falling out, they remained friends throughout elementary school and, as they went to middle school together, agreed they would have each other's backs and help each other navigate the unfamiliar landscape of a school much larger than their intimate elementary school. Lunchtime was especially challenging, with hundreds of adolescents yelling, laughing, and sometimes eating at cramped tables. Jefferson Williams arrived first and not knowing where to sit, took a place at a table where the other Black students were. Nobody offered to talk with him, but that was OK because he knew that Jefferson Thomas would soon be there. As soon as Thomas walked in, Williams yelled, *"Over here, Jefferson!"* Pizza and milk in hand, Thomas joined his friend, not realizing until he sat down that he was the only white student at the table. He heard a few giggles and laughs that appeared to be aimed toward him, but the first day of middle school was unnerving enough without getting into any conflicts, especially if he didn't even know if they were conflicts. The boys hurriedly ate their meal and didn't say much. *"How was algebra?"* *"OK. How was science?"* And so the conversation went until the bell rang, signaling it was time to join the crowded hallways to try to find the next class. As they passed a table of older boys, Thomas heard the not-so-subtle command, *"Next time, sit here."* A brief chorus of boys singing followed: *"On the good ship Amistad"* to the tune of *"On the Good Ship Lollipop."* Another said something else, but the word boy *was unmistakable, dripping with contempt toward Williams. Both boys walked wordlessly to the hallway.* *"Later,"* said the Jeffersons in unison. *The first day of middle school was only half over, but something didn't feel right. Both boys were upset and distracted throughout the afternoon.*

Discussion questions: Should Williams have said anything at being called "boy"? Should Thomas have turned around and challenged the students who were taunting them? Should they have discussed the incident with a teacher? Should they discuss it with their parents when, inevitably, their parents ask, "What happened in school today?"

Roots of a Name

Savannah Jackson had been raised to be proud of her heritage. Her father was publisher of the weekly paper the Mercury, *which was run by the fourth generation of Jacksons. Once it had been a thriving daily paper that Black-owned businesses in the late 1800s and throughout the 20th century supported. It was a leading voice against Jim Crow and for the civil rights movement, and also editorialized on local issues including water pollution, education, and city council districting. Andrew Jackson had a journalism degree from Columbia University and could have worked for any paper in the nation, including the* New York Times, *his dream job. But when his father became ill, Mr. Jackson came back to run the* Mercury. *Seeing advertising revenue decline and more readers move to web-based sources for news, he changed the format of the print edition to weekly and started an online newspaper from scratch. As his readership aged, he faced simultaneous complaints from loyal readers who told him that "Your father gave us the paper every day" to those who said, "If you don't get into the 21st century and translate these ad dollars into revenues, I can't buy ads from you anymore." It was not a fun time to be a newspaper owner. But every day, at precisely 6:30 p.m., Mr. Jackson sat down to his favorite part of the day, the family dinner. The television was turned off, calls were unanswered, and no electronic devices were allowed at the dinner table. They used the best china because, Mrs. Jackson explained to startled dinner guests, when she and Mr. Jackson were first married, those two china pieces were the only plates in the house. So, from the time they lived in a studio apartment to today, when their family of six sat down in a lovely dining room, they still used the same china to remind them of those early days. The dinners always included not only a rundown of the school day but also lively discussions and debates, and Mr. and Mrs. Jackson presided as impartial judges among the four children.*

This evening, however, was different. "Daddy," Savannah began, "I hate my name." Mr. Jackson, always a cool presence at the heart of a storm, did not react in anger but said, "Honey, that's a proud name—your grandmother's name." "It's a slave name, Daddy. And honestly, I don't like the Jackson part either." Now it was Mrs. Jackson's turn. "Our family name has been in this town for generations. When you were a little baby, people would say, 'Yes, she's a Jackson, all right,' and that always made us so proud. What's wrong, baby?" Savannah was not just another disgruntled teenager. She had never received a grade other than an A, was the favorite to be the high school valedictorian, and had her sights set on Columbia, where her father had gone. She continued, "I don't want to go to college with a first name from a slave market and a last name from a slave master. I just hate my name!"

There was a long pause. Mr. Jackson knew friends who brooked no dissent from their teenage children, but that intransigence invariably led to rebellion. He didn't want to be like one of those drill sergeant dads, but this conversation wounded him deeply. Determined not to raise his voice, he said, "Savannah, you know we love you more than life itself. This is your name. I'm sorry that you don't like it right now, but it's the name that you and your family bear. We bear it proudly." Savannah pulled out an envelope from her pocket, unfolded a paper, and presented it to her father. "Daddy, this is a legal application for a change of name. I want to be known as Nofoto X. Nofoto is a Zulu name for 'like her grandmother.' You see, Daddy, I want to honor my grandmother with a name that is not Savannah. X honors the American civil rights warrior Malcolm X. We just read his autobiography in class, and I think you might have had something to do with that." Mr. Jackson got the point. His newspaper had editorialized in favor of more Black studies in the high school, and he had personally appeared before the school board arguing that the absence of these subjects was historically wrong and represented educational malpractice. His daughter benefited from this curriculum, and now he had to think about how to respond to the young adult sitting at his dinner table whom he still called "Baby." "You can refuse to sign it if you want, Daddy, but the day I turn eighteen, I'm making the change. I'd like to have your approval, but I won't wait for it."

Discussion question: What should the Jackson family do?

Conclusion

Discussions about race and racism are difficult within the same family, as the Jacksons are learning. There are many people who want to be sympathetic to the cause of racial justice but believe sincerely that they are not responsible for injustice because it is not their fault. That is the challenge we take up in the next chapter.

CHAPTER 8

Talking About Action: How Can Something Be My Responsibility When It's Not My Fault?

In the classic book *The Road Less Traveled*, psychiatrist M. Scott Peck (1978/2002) suggests that there is never a perfect assumption of responsibility. We can assume too much responsibility—everything is my fault, from the weather, to my parents, to the behavior of others—in which case we are neurotic. Or we can assume too little responsibility—nothing is my fault, and I am blameless for the conditions of others—in which case we have a character defect. While neither condition is ideal, Peck (1978/2002) suggests that it is a lot easier to treat neuroses than character defects. Early in our children's lives, we teach them to "be responsible," meaning that they understand their actions and how those actions affect others. But as children age, they begin to understand that responsibility extends beyond their own actions to their friends, neighborhood, school, and the world at large. When children see litter on the street, we teach them to dispose of it, not because they left the litter or it is their fault that the paper is on the sidewalk, but rather because we are all responsible for keeping our neighborhood clean. When they see another child crying, even very young children may seek to console the child, not because they caused the distress but because they have empathy for a stranger who is hurting. It is the impulse that often leads older children and adults to intervene when a child is being bullied, attempt to save someone who is drowning, or defend a colleague who is being mistreated. This is what decent human beings do—they share responsibility for the world around them and seek to right wrongs, even when they did not directly cause those wrongs. Empathy, responsibility, and associated actions are the glue that holds civil society together. In this chapter, we consider the meaning of responsibility and how it differs from fault. Mindful of Peck's (1978/2002) continuum of character defects to neuroses, we seek to take reasonable amounts of responsibility without sinking into irredeemable despair. Responsibility is at the heart of challenging conversations about race, because while no reader of this book owned slaves, many of us benefit from the heritage of slave ownership. Slavery in the 19th century was not our fault, but we struggle to come to grips with our responsibility in the 21st century.

The Meaning of Responsibility

Educators often confront factors influencing student achievement that are far beyond their control. Students failed to learn essential skills in the previous year. Students came to school bleary-eyed, malnourished, or stoned. During the school closures associated with the COVID-19 pandemic, some students fell far behind their economically advantaged peers because they lacked access to technology that was their only source of learning. In brief, the world of education is full of factors beyond the school of teachers and administrators, and thus we are not responsible for the past. Where then does our responsibility lie? With things we can control, and most importantly, with things that we can influence to help students in the future (Ye, 2018). In the wryly titled essay "It's Not My Fault I Never Learned to Accept Responsibility," business consultant Gary Korisko (n.d.) makes the case that taking responsibility, including responsibility for factors beyond our control, is far more empowering than bewailing the fact that bad things happen. Resilience, a key characteristic for success in school and in life, depends in large part on our ability to focus on the factors, however slight, that are within our control and to concentrate our mental energies there (Chowdhury, 2020). Every moment we devote to finding fault and looking for the guilty party is one we cannot devote to repair of the present and hope for the future.

As of this writing, we do not know what caused the COVID-19 pandemic. All we can control is our own response to it. The same is true with natural disasters, broken relationships, job failures, and academic disappointments. While finding fault may provide some psychic relief in the short run by absolving us of personal guilt, it is generally an unworthy expenditure of time and emotional energy.

Adult Choices in Fault and Responsibility

We expect rational adults to distinguish between fault and responsibility. It is not the fault of any reader that fossil fuels were in wide and growing use long before we were born. We are not responsible for factors we could not control. But it is our fault if, knowing the dangers of fossil fuels, we persist in using them. As recently as the 1950s, physicians were recommending cigarettes to pregnant women, and those who followed the advice of their doctors were not responsible for the consequences (Harford, 2021). But today we know better, and the choice to smoke endangers not only oneself but also the lives of those around you. Previous generations in the United States were told that Native Americans were savages or that Japanese Americans needed to be interned for the country's safety. Yet most Americans today recognize that both were lies. Similarly, current Americans did not personally evict the original inhabitants of North America from their lands, but they derive undeniable benefits from this displacement every day. We citizens of the 21st century did not invent the institution of slavery or consciously seek to benefit from it, but to say that we bear no responsibility for benefits and the hardships imposed on others is to deny reality.

Scenarios About Fault and Responsibility

These scenarios can be used in classrooms or other discussion groups, with the first one especially helpful for elementary school students, teachers, and parents. The second scenario should be considered as a spur to faculty discussion, especially if the faculty is considering engaging in equity and anti-racism professional learning experiences.

A Bad Word

"Timmy said a bad word," Camille told her second-grade teacher. "Really? What was that?" replied Ms. Horowitz. She loved teaching second grade,

an age of wonder and learning when students start to express themselves and find a voice. Students in second grade could be creative and sometimes a bit histrionic—everything was either a magical event or a tearful failure—but Ms. Horowitz and her endless supply of tissues managed to get through every day with more laughter than tears as she built students who could confidently go on to third grade. "It was a really, really bad word," persisted Camille. "OK, why don't you tell me?" asked Ms. Horowitz. "I can't," replied Camille, her voice trailing off. "Would you write it down for me?" Tentatively taking a pencil and paper, Camille wrote the N-word. While Ms. Horowitz generally discouraged tattling, she knew she needed to address this. She was also perplexed because Timmy was kind, thoughtful, and a very advanced reader. To her way of thinking, only unkind and uneducated people used that word. He would never, thought Ms. Horowitz, do something intentionally hurtful and certainly gave no indications that he or his parents were racists. Where in the world did this come from?

At the next recess, Ms. Horowitz asked Timmy to stay for a moment. "I have a question I'd like to ask you, Timmy, and I need you to answer honestly. I'm going to show you a word, and I want to know if you are saying it." She wrote the N-word in her neat printing and handed it to Timmy. "Yes!" Timmy said eagerly. "My brother and I watched the 'Freaky Friday' video, and it was really funny. I sang the song on the playground and everybody laughed. Wait, did I do something wrong? Am I in trouble?" Timmy's lip started to quiver. He had never been in trouble at school, and his parents were always proud of him, especially the way that his teachers said he was a good helper, friend, and student. "You're not in trouble," Ms. Horowitz said, "but you did say a very bad word, and I don't want you to say it again."

"Are you going to call my parents?" asked Timmy. "Am I going to have to go to the principal's office? It's not my fault! I was just copying my brother." Timmy had never been to the principal's office, but he knew it was a place where students went when they had done something truly awful. "I'm not going to call your parents, and you don't have to go to the principal's office," Ms. Horowitz assured him. "But I don't want you to use this word ever again. Is that clear?" "Yes, ma'am," Timmy said. "Can I go to the playground now?"

Discussion questions: How did Ms. Horowitz handle this situation? What, if anything, should

she do next? Should she talk with the parents
or the principal?

Another Racism Workshop

"If I hear another word about racism," said Mr. Leonard, the revered high school football coach, "I'm going to explode." He had just emerged from one in a twelve-part series of anti-racism trainings the district required and had heard all he could take. Mr. Leonard had abandoned a business career to teach in an inner-city school and devoted not only his professional life but also much of his personal time to mentoring students. After decades of supporting inner-city youth, he didn't need a lecture about racism from someone with an Ivy League pedigree wearing a Chanel suit. Speaking to no one in particular, he fumed, "For more than twenty years, I've been opening the doors to college for my players, most of whom are African American. The lessons they learned on the field are what helped them stay in school and succeed in class both here and in college. They succeeded because I was tough, not because I felt sorry for them. Ask them—they'll tell you it was discipline, hard work, and team loyalty that led to five state championships, a 100 percent high school graduation rate, and millions of dollars in college scholarships. Heck, I've had Black kids stay in my home when things were not going well for them with their parents. And today, a white lady with a fancy suit is telling me that I'm a racist. I just can't take this anymore." Dr. Pembroke, the principal, overheard the coach and asked him if he wanted to talk. The two had always been close, and Dr. Pembroke had served as the coach before going into administration. He knew the long hours and sacrifices that coaches made, not just to win games but to meet the personal needs of many players. "I haven't asked for many favors, Doc," Mr. Leonard began, "but you've got to get me out of these workshops. They're just not fair, and it makes me feel like all that I've done for these kids doesn't mean a thing." Dr. Pembroke could tell how upset the coach was and suggested they take a walk around the field where they could speak privately. "Coach," he began, "you know that I've stuck up for you and the program plenty of times. And that includes some really awful situations in which our African American athletes were threatened and intimidated. Nooses in the locker room? That would have gotten a lot of coaches fired." "C'mon, Doc," countered the coach. "You know I didn't have anything to do with that. It wasn't my fault, and

to this day I don't know who did it." "That's right," said the principal. "That incident was not your fault, but what happens in the locker room is your responsibility. It suggests what students think you will tolerate, and because we never found the perpetrators and never held anyone accountable, we have some racists in this school who got away with despicable behavior." "I still don't understand how these workshops help anything. The kids who need to be in these workshops are the kids who are doing bad things to my players. I'm not the one who needs to hear that message." "Well, Coach, what message is it that you don't want to hear?" "I don't want to hear," said Coach Leonard through gritted teeth, "that I'm a no-good racist who doesn't care about his kids." "That's not what I heard at all in the workshop," replied the principal. "We've got a real problem in this school. I know that you get the students to make nice and play together on the field, but look at the cafeteria, look in the hallways. Heck, look in the classrooms. We're as segregated now as we were fifty years ago." "Perhaps so," said the coach, "but all I know is that it's not my fault, and I don't want to sit through another gripe session with that lady."

> ### Discussion question: What should the principal do?

Conclusion

In this chapter, we explored fault and responsibility. Young students can give grave offense, however unintentionally, because they don't know how words can hurt. Adults, as well, can be sensitive when they mistake the acknowledgment of collective responsibility for an accusation of personal guilt. We considered how volatile, in fact, a discussion can become when dedicated professionals interpret discussions about racism as personal indictments. In the next chapter, we move to our affirmative duties for fairness and justice, including advocacy and individual commitments.

CHAPTER 9

Talking About Advocacy: What Is My Duty to My Friends?

R osa Isiah brings her perspective as an educator and leader who has seen advocacy done well and done badly at every level. She helps us understand that our duty for advocacy is neither abstract nor something that happens only in legislative chambers but rather something that can happen in every school at every level.

The protests and unrest that occurred after the murder of George Floyd in Minneapolis in May 2020 moved many from silence to actionable and vocal support for change. The tragedy of those nine minutes and twenty-nine seconds compelled thousands worldwide to stand in solidarity with the Black community and fueled a movement for change against racism and police brutality. Most middle-class white families have not witnessed this level of unrest and injustice in their lives. Yes, the children are watching, and they are not OK.

Students need age-appropriate opportunities to discuss and make meaning of tragic events and topics that impact their daily lives and relationships with others. Race, racism, injustice, and inequity, to name a powerful few, impact the lives of people of color daily. Younger students may not have the words to describe this level of injustice or systemic oppression, but if you listen deeply, it is clear they are concerned about these complex societal issues. Opportunities to think critically about these issues and how to resolve them need to be part of the learning we provide in our schools at every level. After all, is it not our responsibility to help develop critical thinkers, problem solvers, and empathetic scholars?

Many educators are unsure about what to say or how to say it; this is normal. Many are uncomfortable with or fearful of their roles as educators who advocate for equity; this is also normal. The truth is, we do not have the luxury of waiting for adult comfort levels to rise before we engage in advocacy for change. Our students are already having the conversations we shy away from, and they need guidance. Lives depend on it.

The Meaning of *Advocacy*

The basic meaning of *advocacy*, as *Merriam-Webster* defines it, is the "act or process of supporting a cause or proposal: the act or process of advocating something" ("Advocacy," n.d.). By definition, advocacy is about an act or action. An advocate is someone who actively supports and promotes a cause. When we advocate, we declare our solidarity and do everything we can to create change. We have advocates in education, but as education researcher John Hattie shares with us, the most influential impact on student achievement is the teacher in the classroom (Hattie & Yates, 2014). Your ability to teach and lead as educators for advocacy and social change is needed today, more than ever. Yes, students have questions.

Scenarios About Advocacy

You can begin the challenging conversations about race and advocacy at any grade level using scenarios across grade spans, including elementary. Let's consider the three scenarios in this chapter. The first scenario, Is That Fair?, explores the awakening that some students experience when they realize that not all people are treated fairly. The second scenario, One Size Does Not Fit All, considers the implications of grouping all Hispanic or all English learners into one category. The third scenario, Should I Say Something?, illustrates the courage it takes to speak up for others when things don't make sense. The last scenario, Are My Parents Right?, is about realizing that you may not understand or align with the belief system you are immersed in.

Is That Fair?

Miguel was fed up with being treated differently for not speaking English very well. He was new to California from Peru and was learning to speak

English. He learned enough conversational English to understand that Mike, his fourth-grade classmate, often made fun of the Hispanic students. He teased and picked on them. He called them names and told them to "go back to Mexico." This made Miguel and other students angry, but the majority of students remained silent, and the teachers never reprimanded Mike for his rude comments and bullying behavior. One day after lunch, Miguel heard Mike whisper to his friends, "There goes another one . . . he needs to speak English or leave. Maybe we need a wall around here to keep them out." Mike picked up a french fry from the trash can and threw it at Miguel, hitting him in the face. Miguel felt the anger rush to his fists. He was furious and couldn't take it anymore. Miguel dropped his backpack and tackled Mike to the ground. "Get this Mexican off me!" yelled Mike. The school principal heard the fight and quickly ran over to separate them. Miguel and Mike met with the principal, and they both had a chance to share what happened. Mike lied about what he did to Miguel and to other Hispanic students. The principal, Mr. Smith, scolded Miguel and suspended him two days for fighting. Mr. Smith gave Mike a warning and sent him back to class.

Discussion questions: Were the consequences that Miguel and Mike received fair? Why do you think Mike wasn't suspended from school? Why do you think other students kept quiet about Mike's behavior toward Hispanic students? What do you think Miguel and students like Miguel should do about the way students like Mike bully them?

One Size Does Not Fit All

Lincoln Middle School was located in the heart of Los Angeles, California. Lincoln was a Title I high-poverty school with more than 80 percent of students having a low socioeconomic status. The majority, or 75 percent, of the students at Lincoln were Hispanic. Most of the Hispanic students at Lincoln were second- or third-generation Americans whose parents had also attended Lincoln as young teenagers. Many of these students and parents were not fluent English or Spanish speakers, and some students in this category were classified as English learners, accounting for 30 percent of Lincoln's students.

Ms. Perez was a seventh-grade teacher at Lincoln. She loved her work with all students, but especially students who were new to U.S. schools. Ms. Perez had grown up in Mexico and immigrated to the United States as a young child, so she related to the experiences of those students. As the English department chairperson, Ms. Perez struggled to grow her department's understanding of language acquisition and culturally responsive pedagogy.

The principal at Lincoln, Ms. L., was one of the educators who Ms. Perez wanted to reach. Ms. L. often shared that she worked at a school with 75 percent English learners, failing to understand that Hispanic *did not equate to* English learner. *Ms. L. shared this statement with parents, teachers, and others who questioned the academic progress at Lincoln. Ms. Perez was bothered by this and attempted to provide the principal with accurate information, as the principal's lack of understanding of her Hispanic student population often led to misidentification of student needs, inadequate allocation of human and fiscal resources, and inapplicable professional development topics for teachers. Ms. Perez wondered whether the principal's beliefs also impacted the teaching staff's expectations of Hispanic students at Lincoln.*

The lack of knowledge about the diverse Hispanic student population at Lincoln was an issue across content areas. Teachers did the best they could, but they lacked a real understanding of who their students were. Yes, 75 percent of students were Hispanic, but only 30 percent of the students at Lincoln were classified English learners as measured by California's yearly English learner proficiency assessment. Hispanic students and Hispanic English learners at Lincoln were falling behind, and change would require more than what Ms. Perez alone could achieve.

Discussion questions: What are the implications of misunderstanding the unique needs of Hispanic students and English learners? What might Ms. Perez begin to do to educate her principal and her colleagues

about the academic needs of Hispanic
students at Lincoln Middle School?

Should I Say Something?

*Linda loved her middle school best friend, Pete. Linda was white, and
Pete was black, but despite their differences in race and background, they
had so much in common. They especially enjoyed movies, game shows, and
music. Linda could remember the day Pete came out to her. "I think I'm gay,
Linda . . . do you still want to be my friend?" "Being gay is not a disease!
Of course I'm still your friend," said Linda. As a sixth grader, Pete didn't
feel comfortable sharing how he felt with his parents yet. Pete believed they
would never approve. Some kids at school were judgmental enough about
his race, and he was worried about being bullied. Linda was glad he felt
comfortable enough with her to share.*

*A few weeks later, Linda noticed that Pete was skipping his physical edu-
cation class. She knew it would hurt his grades and asked Pete about it. "I
can't go back to PE class, Linda. I just can't," he said. Linda asked repeatedly
until Pete finally opened up. "Two seventh graders, Josh and Lucas, asked
me if I was gay and threatened to beat me up if I was," Pete said. Linda had
grown up with Josh and was shocked that he would do something like this
to Pete. "They tore up my PE shirt, called me the N-word, and wrote gay
all over my locker with a red permanent marker. The coach knows about it,
and I'm so afraid he'll tell my parents. Please promise me you won't say a
word about this! Please, Linda," he begged. She could see the fear in Pete's
eyes and didn't know what he was more afraid of—his parents or the kids
who'd bullied him.*

Discussion questions: Should Linda talk to
Pete's parents? Should Linda talk to the coach
about what Josh and Lucas did to Pete? What
can Linda do to advocate for her friend? Is
Pete doing the right thing by not telling his
parents about what happened to him?

Are My Parents Right?

Kristy was new to Johnson Elementary School. It was hard to leave her school in the middle of fourth grade, but her parents had to move for work. Kristy liked this school much more than her previous one. Johnson students were not like the students in her last school. They spoke many different languages, and some came from other countries. Kristy loved learning words in new languages and about diverse cultures, foods, and customs. She made friends with a girl named Sasha soon after enrolling at Johnson. Sasha was the first Black friend that Kristy ever had, and she couldn't wait to invite her over to her house to meet her puppy and hang out. Kristy's mom and dad were happy she had made a friend.

Kristy asked if she could have a playdate with Sasha. Kristy's parents agreed and decided to have Sasha over. The next day, Kristy's father picked her up from school. He noticed Sasha standing next to Kristy and asked, "Who is that girl?" Kristy told him all about Sasha and said, "Thank you for agreeing to have Sasha come over, Dad." Kristy's father suddenly got very quiet. He turned and told Kristy, "I don't think it's a good idea to have Sasha over after all." Kristy's heart dropped. She couldn't understand why. She begged and pleaded with both her mom and dad, but they didn't listen. Kristy was confused and upset. When she told Sasha about it, Sasha asked, "Why don't they want me to come over?" "Because my father said so," Kristy replied.

> Discussion questions: Why do you think Kristy's father changed his mind about having Sasha over for a playdate after meeting her? How do you think Sasha felt when Kristy said that her father and mother would not allow Sasha to come over? How can Kristy maintain her friendship despite her parents' disapproval?

Conclusion

Rich learning opportunities and academic achievement for marginalized students depend on our ability to advocate for equity in education. Advocacy—identifying a cause and acting on it—can be a tremendously powerful tool for change and the dismantling of systemic racism. As we work to do this, we can help students find their own self-advocacy voices by practicing empathy and supporting others. This important work can begin through the use of strategies like role playing, vignettes, and scenarios. The scenarios offered in these chapters are great starting points. They will equip you with opportunities to engage students in targeted questions and discussions. Now is the time to lead the learning in your classrooms as educators for social change and social justice.

CHAPTER 10

Talking About Law Enforcement: How Do Police Officers Help Us? How Do They Sometimes Hurt Us?

Ken Williams is the son of a police officer. One of the highlights of his childhood was watching his dad play softball on the department team. Ken recalled that if he had to choose between a Yankees game and watching his dad play, it was not a close call. On the team were other men who Ken thought of as his "uncles" from Irish, Italian, Venezuelan, and many other backgrounds. Ken also called them uncles because, he realized as he grew up, these were the only police officers he had been around where he did not feel some anxiety. He found common ground with them knowing that his father shared their space, mission, games, and commitments. As he grew older, he learned that being the son of a police officer did not insulate him from being pulled over as a result of driving while Black or being fearful when he was at a store counter without his wallet. He is professionally successful, has a great family, and is an internationally recognized author. He has beautifully restored classic cars. But once he drives down Peachtree Street in Atlanta, he's one more Black man driving a car that doesn't quite fit the prevailing expectations of the white residents of that neighborhood—a fact that has critical implications for policing and public safety, which we will explore before considering related scenarios.

Safety for Some

Just as schools are designed perfectly to provide achievement for only some, many community safety organizations are designed to provide safety for only some. This is reflected in the patterns of patrolling, the viability of officers on the beat, and the nature of contacts with the public. While it is easy to demonize police officers who would kneel on the neck of George Floyd and do so while looking directly into the camera, it is more difficult to find the demons in the systems of everyday practice. A classic, but by no means exceptional, example of a system with obvious racial disparities was the stop-and-frisk policy in New York, in which police officers would use mystical insight and suspicion to stop people. Not surprisingly, though Black and Latinx people were 50 percent of the population at the height of the policy, they accounted for 84 percent of the stops (Thompson, 2013). But isn't that because Black and Brown people committed more crimes? The city's own data reveal that for suspects caught with weapons—presumably the reason justifying a frisk—Black suspects were one-half as likely as white suspects to have a weapon. Though courts later ruled the policy unconstitutional, during his 2016 presidential campaign, Donald Trump called to expand the policy from New York to the entire nation (Nelson, 2016).

The relationship between schools and public safety is similar not only in the expectation of disparities but also in their justification. We do not demonize teachers in underperforming schools because we know that many of them appear to be doing heroic work under difficult to impossible conditions. They cannot, after all, undo in six hours a day what is happening in their students' homes, streets, and neighborhoods the rest of the day. Similarly, police departments have been expected to provide social work, counseling, and crisis intervention for which they are ill prepared, and so—just like teachers—we go to great lengths to celebrate the heroes without ever addressing the reasons that we need heroes in the first place. The hero-dependent system may feel good as the bands play and the politicians give speeches, but it never addresses the underlying policies and conditions that made it necessary to depend on heroes.

From Stop and Frisk to Stop *At Risk*

In chapter 1 (page 11), Ken challenged us to consider how the label of a student changed our perceptions and prescriptions. When the student bore the label *at risk*, our perceptions gravitated toward conditions we cannot control, including the student's home life and all that happened outside of school and before the current school year. When the label was changed to *underserved*, the perceptions changed to things we can control, including a broad range of educational, nutritional, and mental and physical health supports. This suggests an opening to more constructive conversations with law enforcement officials. Ken remains an optimist despite being racially profiled. Just as he saw his father succeed as a police officer, Ken knows that officers and community members can succeed in making law enforcement a partnership rather than a confrontation. Moreover, just as there is a context in schools that includes the heritage of segregation and the destructive results to this day of inequities in access to advanced classes, the remedies require recognition, a willingness to confront facts, and institutional changes.

When we consider the pervasive sources of racial injustice in the criminal justice system, it is helpful to understand that some of these injustices are not about white fragility or Black guilt but about human overconfidence in our judgments. For example, most people have great confidence in eyewitness testimony, whether they are members of a jury listening to that testimony or a crime victim providing it. The cinematic portrait of the courageous witness pointing a finger at the defendant and saying, "That's the man who did it. I would never forget that face," turns out to be simply wrong. It's not that the witness is a calculated liar but rather that facial identification, especially of people of different races, is wildly inaccurate. In studies of identification by white and Asian witnesses of Black men in lineups, error rates were little better than chance, while the perception of the accuracy of those lineup identifications was that they were nearly flawless (Eberhardt, 2019). After all, if we are going to deprive you of your liberty, destroy your family, and deliver a lifetime of financial consequences including the inability to get a job, vote, or rent an apartment—all potential consequences of a felony conviction— then we had better be pretty darn sure about identification. The same is true of Black witnesses who attempted to identify Asian perpetrators of a crime. This research was apparently studied by Asian gangs in San Francisco, who used the inability of many Black witnesses to identify them to focus their crimes on Black neighborhoods (Eberhardt, 2019). This is not, in brief, an indictment of police officers, but rather of the system on which they depend and their persistent overreliance on the testimony of witnesses who are not as accurate as they claim to be.

Scenarios About Policing

In the following scenarios, students respond to situations with fear, reflecting their perceptions not just of law enforcement but of society at large. As you read the story of Shawna, consider how you might react in the same situation. Consider, too, why Malcolm and Jordan react so differently to the same situation.

Shawna's Purse

Shawna's family didn't have a lot of money, so she learned at an early age that the money she earned should be safeguarded wisely. Although she was only ten, she already had her own bank account. Shawna walked dogs, served as a "Mama's helper," and even helped younger kids read. She did messy and unpleasant work, such as cleaning up apartments in the neighborhood when somebody moved out or was evicted. She didn't always get paid, but when she did, she would save money, buy a present for her mom, give some to church, and occasionally spend something for herself. Shawna's grandmother was so proud of her granddaughter's work ethic that she gave her a beautiful coin purse for her birthday. It was decorated and even had a light so that she could see the contents in the dark.

In the winter, the walk home from the bus stop was cold and dark, and Shawna always followed her mother's instructions to go straight home. One day, as she held her books in one hand and her purse in the other, she felt a shove and was down on the pavement. When she got up, she had her books, but her purse, and the seven dollars and seventy cents inside, were gone. She was devastated, and crawled around on the sidewalk, ground, and street trying to find her purse. Seeing her distress, a police officer pulled up in a car and asked, "What are you doing in the street? You could get hurt!" Shawna froze, and then ran home, tears streaming down her face. She was afraid that the police might be chasing her, so she ran faster and faster until she burst into her apartment, sat on the floor, and wept. She didn't know what to say or do.

Discussion questions: What should Shawna tell her mother? What might she have said to the police officer? What would you do if the same thing happened to you?

Malcolm's Comic Book

Malcolm loved comic books. An avid reader since first grade, he was willing to read chapter books and was proud of the fact that his teacher regarded him as a good reader, but whenever he had the chance and the money to buy the latest superhero comic, he jumped at it. Malcolm's friend, Jordan, also enjoyed comics. Sometimes they would read and reread them together until they knew the dialogue by heart. But after a while, when they had memorized every word of a book, they were bored and wanted another one. Neither boy's family had much money or gave an allowance, but even without money, they would go to the drug store and thumb through the latest comics. One day, one of the store employees noticed that the boys were looking through the comics without buying them. It looked as if the plastic seal package had been broken, and the employee said sternly, "This isn't a library. If you want these comics, you have to pay for them." Though both boys were looking at the comics, it was clear that the store employee was directing his anger toward Jordan, who was Black. While Jordan received the warning, red-haired Malcolm deftly placed a comic book under his shirt and walked past saying, "See you later, Jordan!"

When the two boys met outside, Malcolm revealed his prize, the stolen comic book. "Pretty cool, right?" asked Malcolm. But a look of terror came over Jordan's face. "If I get caught with that, I will go to jail!" "OK, OK," said Malcolm, "I'll take it back if you want." "No," pleaded Jordan. "I'm the one they will suspect, and then they will think I'm the thief, and I will be in more trouble than you can understand. I seriously, really, probably, will go to jail." And with that, Jordan started running away from his former friend as fast as he could.

> Discussion questions: Should Jordan and Malcolm have returned the comic to the store? Was Jordan's fear real or an exaggeration? Was the store employee acting appropriately?

Kenneth and the Cafeteria Money

Being trusted to sell snack cakes and sodas was a big responsibility for an eighth grader at his Catholic school. Kenneth had proven himself to be a responsible young man, and so Mrs. Clark gave him this duty. Wandering the narrow spaces in the parochial school cafeteria, full of noise and constant motion, was tricky, but Kenneth handled it with ease, turning in the money and any remaining sodas and snack cakes to Mrs. Clark. But after a while, Kenneth found the temptation to first take a bite out of a cake, and then the whole cake, too tempting to resist. After all, Mrs. Clark didn't appear to actually count any of the merchandise, but only collected the sodas, snack cakes, and quarters when Kenneth had finished his rounds. Before too long, it was not just a cake that was missing, but some sodas and eventually some quarters as well. But it turned out that Mrs. Clark had been counting the goods and the money every day and caught Kenneth in his theft. She gave the assignment to another student, leaving Kenneth deeply embarrassed and ashamed. After a few months, however, Mrs. Clark gave Kenneth another chance. "She had no reason to trust me," Kenneth recalled years later, "but Mrs. Clark thought I deserved another chance. I'll never forget that."

> Discussion questions: Was Mrs. Clark right to give Kenneth a second chance? Why do you think she was so kind to Kenneth even though he made such a mistake?

Into the Wall

"What happened to you?" asked the assistant principal, Mr. Joyner, who made a point of greeting students as they got off the bus and entered Jefferson Davis High School. "Nothing," replied Marcus, pulling his cap farther down

on his head. "Hey, no hats in the building!" called a counselor, standing her ground at her appointed place in the hallway. Marcus removed his cap and moved into his usual chair in the last row of his algebra class, putting his head on his desk. The students at Davis had an unspoken agreement with many teachers: "We won't make you work too hard if you don't make us work too hard." Although he had been student council president in his middle school, Marcus found high school to be much rougher. Many students didn't know him, he didn't really know his teachers except to understand how overworked they were, and unlike middle school, no counselor ever checked in on him. So, he was surprised when the counselor came to the algebra class, went directly to his desk, and said, "Come with me." Marcus followed her down the hallway and into her tiny office.

"So," the counselor began, "tell me what happened." "Nothing happened," said Marcus clearly. "It looks to me like you were beat up pretty good, and I've been doing this long enough to tell the difference between the marks left by fists and those left by a club. Marcus, were you hit by a cop?" "I told you," Marcus said firmly, "nothing happened." "Listen," said the counselor with a gentler tone than before, "you're not the first student in this school who was beat up by a cop, and if you don't help me, you won't be the last. This school is a lot less segregated than when I graduated forty-two years ago, but you're still a young Black man in a community where the police force is more than 80 percent white. Young men like you get beat up, and reporting harassment and abuse can get those officers off the street."

"Look, Miss," Marcus said quietly. "You don't know what it's like. Those cops know where I live. They drive by my house every day and night. I've got two little brothers and a sister, and I can't get them in trouble. I can take a beating. They can't." "But, Marcus," the counselor persisted, "you don't have to take a beating. I can help you. Please tell me at least a little bit." "OK, Miss, I'll tell you," Marcus said, his voice rising. "I saw this cop beat the crap out of my friend Elijah. I don't know why, but I know that as soon as the cop saw that I had been a witness, he and his buddies came to me, and after he hit me a few times with his stick, he asked if I had seen anything." "And what did you say to the officer?" asked the counselor. "I said, 'No, sir, I didn't see anything.' And then he hit me again and walked away." "My God!" said the counselor. "You have to tell me who did this." "No, Miss, I don't." And with that, Marcus got up and returned to class.

Discussion questions: What should the counselor do? What should Marcus do? What can students, teachers, and administrators do? Why do you think Marcus is unwilling to cooperate with the counselor and to stop further police abuse?

The Colonel and the Chief

Shakira Madison was the pride of her family. Her father, Colonel James Madison, earned the rank in a thirty-year military career that included combat service and numerous decorations for his bravery, leadership, and exceptional service. He enlisted straight out of high school, earned his undergraduate and master's degrees while in the military, and rose from private to colonel. Still trim at forty-eight, he wore his dress blue uniform when making speeches around the state to encourage young people to serve in the military and participate in high school Junior Reserve Officer Training Corps (JROTC). One of his proudest days as a father was when Shakira was selected as commandant of cadets, the first young woman to receive the honor. By day, Colonel Madison was the chief of police in their leafy suburb. While eligible for a full military retirement, he joked that "about two days of retirement was all that I, or Mrs. Madison, could stand." He threw himself into the job, taking the same physical training test demanded of recruits, setting high leadership standards for the sergeants and officers on the force, and, when necessary, disciplining officers who failed to measure up to his expectations. Immediately after the murder of Mr. George Floyd at the hands of police officers in Minneapolis, Colonel Madison requested an urgent meeting with the mayor and city council. "We have to show that the murderers do not reflect real police." He served on the board of many community organizations, including the Congress of Racial Equality, a branch of the Southern Christian Leadership Conference that Dr. Martin Luther King Jr. helped found, and was an elder in his racially mixed church. He was clearly regarded as a leader in the Black community as well as the chief of police.

As Colonel Madison was organizing community events to advocate for peace and racial justice, Shakira had different challenges at school. By the third time classmates whom she considered friends said coolly, "Good morning, Tom," she knew exactly what they meant. Because she was the daughter of the police chief and known as a stickler for following the rules and pursuing academic excellence, at least a few classmates were clearly calling her an Uncle Tom, a person for whom white affiliation was more important than the clarion call to embrace the Black Lives Matter movement. Shakira never lost her cool, but she made two decisions that led to a confrontation she could not foresee. First, she insisted that the JROTC color guard participate in the memorial service for Mr. Floyd and march with students in the Black Lives Matter parade that followed. Second, she met with the principal and asked that the school also host a Blue Lives Matter assembly. She was angry that her father was being portrayed as a bigot cop and she as an Uncle Tom, and she wanted a forum in which to tell her story. The principal listened to her request and said that he would think about it. But the truth was that the principal, always one to avoid conflict, had already made up his mind. "A Blue Lives Matter assembly?" he asked incredulously. "You've got to be kidding. And I'm not too sure I want my students in military uniforms marching with protestors who might turn violent. Let's just lie low and let this whole thing pass over." Shakira knew that her requests were reasonable and had no idea that she was running into a brick wall.

> **Discussion questions: What should the principal do? What should Shakira do if her requests are denied? What should Colonel Madison do? What other options do the students have?**

Conclusion

In this chapter, we considered the challenging issue police officers in society, especially their role in helping—and hurting—Black and Brown students, families, and neighborhoods, present. We seem to have little difficulty finding Black students in detention, special education, the streets, and adult correctional facilities. But one place we don't find them is in groups that represent the financial and college opportunities associated with academic distinction. In the next chapter, we will consider where the Black people are in schools.

CHAPTER 11

Talking About School: Where Are the Black People?

Education is the great equalizer, bringing together students of every economic class and racial background. Since the 1954 U.S. Supreme Court decision *Brown v. Board of Education of Topeka*, the United States officially repudiated the doctrine that segregated schools could be separate but equal because, as the court declared, separate was inherently unequal. So that pretty much solved racism, right? Sixty years after the Brown decision, schools still remain deeply segregated and unequal, according to teacher and journalist Keith Meatto (2019), with more than half of U.S. students in racially concentrated schools. Even in schools that maintain the appearance of integration, with the percentages of children of different races roughly reflecting the racial composition of the community, the reality of racial segregation sets in as soon as the students cross the threshold of the school door. For example, Black and Hispanic students take AP classes, a path toward college-level coursework and expectations, at a rate starkly lower than their percentage of the student population, and the rate of those students who earn a passing score on these exams is even lower (Jaschik, 2019). In this chapter, we explore the roots of these disparities and other racial divisions that occur within schools. The scenarios we consider, from the primary-school classroom to college lecture halls, suggest that laws alone are insufficient to dismantle the structural disadvantages that Black and Brown students face every day. Our purpose is not to cast blame on schools but rather to learn how schools are only a microcosm of racial divisions that occur throughout society.

How Schools Reinforce Society's Values

Since 1836, *McGuffey Readers* have been influential in U.S. education. In the mid-19th century, few students persisted beyond sixth grade, so these textbooks that William Holmes McGuffey edited, formed the basis not only for student literacy but also for their sense of the world. The *McGuffey Readers* not only taught reading, spelling, and grammar but also imparted moral lessons about truth, obedience to one's parents and teachers, Protestant Christian faith, and patriotism (McGuffey, 1879). For more than a century, *McGuffey Readers*' selected stories, poems, and lessons dominated the U.S. educational scene. In the late 20th and early 21st centuries, McGuffey made a comeback in many quarters as a reflection of the demand for the basics of good literacy and high expectations for students (Lynch, 2016). Compare the prose in McGuffey books to those widely used in the 21st century, and the expectation differences are stark. Passages from the fourth-grade *Reader* reflect a Flesch–Kincaid reading level of ninth grade (Reeves, 2010), a laudable characteristic if only we can put aside the absence of any but white faces and voices inside the covers of these books. It's easy to take potshots at antebellum writers who wrote in an age when slave owners and their supporters regarded enslavement of Africans as legal, moral, and normal. But the absence of writers, characters, and settings that reflect a diverse community remains persistent well into the 21st century. As we will discover in the scenarios later in this chapter, students can graduate from elite schools without ever having studied writers other than those with European backgrounds. This is not because of overt racism, as those teaching English, selecting textbooks, and deciding on academic standards for students are no doubt people of goodwill who oppose racism at every turn. Their decisions about what students should learn and, importantly, how to assess them, reflect values that educators hope will open the doors of opportunity to students. In order to gain access to scholarships, higher education, and jobs that will provide personal meaning and financial security, we want students who learn to become conscientious, well-spoken, and hardworking. The lessons from McGuffey take on a hard edge as well, describing children in mortal peril if they are disobedient and dishonest. Deeply ingrained in these writings is the

Protestant work ethic that reflected McGuffey's deep Calvinist faith and, more broadly, a belief that the virtues he extols lead to a life of success and happiness. That leaves the uncomfortable but inescapable conclusion, impressed on very young minds, that the absence of success and happiness is the result of a lack of the self-reliance, intelligence, honesty, and patriotism associated with the good life. It is the essence of meritocracy—if you succeed, you earned it; if you fail, you (and your ancestors) deserved it. This mindset allows the children and the society into which they are born to excuse all manner of inequities as the result of natural determinism and personal decisions, for which we feel pride or shame depending on the outcome. Lest we think this is a product of the unenlightened days before we were aware of *white fragility* (DiAngelo, 2018), the faith in meritocracy remains deeply rooted in society, and it is at the heart of the scenarios in this chapter. Is the solution to fling wide the doors of opportunity and success to more students, or rather to question the very foundations on which those doors are built?

Scenarios About Daily Decisions About Race

It starts in the crib. University of Toronto researcher Kang Lee and his colleagues (as cited in Craig, 2017) find that babies as young as six months old prefer faces of their own race possibly because of lack of exposure to other races. When bias is ingrained at such an early age, it's not difficult to understand why lectures for students and workshops for their teachers about racism are very popular but have little impact (Bergner, 2020). This dilemma is at the heart of daily decisions about race in schools.

Friendship

Ashlee and Jenna have been friends since their toddler days on the playground. They learned to walk, speak, share, and play together. Their parents are filled with joy and a little apprehension about the first day of kindergarten, with clothes picked out the night before, lunches carefully packed, and excited giggles filling the air. Ashlee's mother, who is Black, and Jenna's mother, who is white, are also friends, sharing occasional coffee, dinner, and game nights. While they enjoy each other's company, they are also clear that

part of their agenda is giving their children positive models of racial toler-
ance. They want their daughters to have a better experience than they did
in elementary school, where despite the progressive and tolerant atmosphere,
Black and white kids just didn't spend much time together unless the teachers
required it. Their kids, they knew, would be different.

As soon as they began their walk home from school that first day, the
mothers knew something was wrong. Rather than walking together, each
girl grabbed the arm of her mother and walked quickly, clearly wanting
to go home. When asked what was wrong, both girls said "nothing" and
continued their urgent pace. As soon as the door closed behind her, Jenna
burst into tears and shouted, "Ashlee doesn't like me anymore! What's
wrong with me? I didn't do anything!" At Ashlee's home, a similar scene
played out, with the new kindergartener sobbing, "All I did was talk with
my friends, and Ashlee thought I didn't want to be her friend anymore. I
hate school." It didn't take long to sort out what had happened at school.
Ashlee hadn't seen some of her friends all summer long, and as soon as she
saw them, she left Jenna's side to exchange animated stories about sum-
mer. These conversations continued at recess and lunch, with Ashlee paying
attention to her friends, most of whom were Black, and Jenna wonder-
ing if she had done something wrong to lead to her exclusion from the
group. In both houses, the dinner conversation began as it would for the
next thirteen years: "What happened in school today?" The reply from both
girls: "Nothing."

> Discussion questions: The parents want the
> next day to be better for both girls. What
> should they do? On the one hand, they
> have raised their daughters to be their own
> advocates, and they have been critical of
> supermoms who swoop in to save their child
> from every disappointment. On the other
> hand, they are anguished over a bad start
> to the school year. Should they talk to the

teachers, the principal, or other parents? What
should they say to their daughters?

Review of Class Reading

*Mary slammed her books down on the kitchen table, usually a place of
quiet study for this straight A, precocious sixteen-year-old. She was the
responsible one in her group, and her friends teasingly called her "Mom"
because she was the one who organized events, helped them with homework,
and could always be counted on to get things done. "What in the world is
wrong?" her dad asked, surprised at this outburst of anger from his normally
placid daughter. "Did you know," she began, "that I can graduate from this
school and never read a single African American author? This place is racist
with a capital R," she declared. "Wait a minute, lovey," her father interrupted. "You read a lot of African American writers and have since you were
a little kid." "Right," Mary responded, "but that's because I chose to read
them—it was never required. My friends can get the same grades I get and
never have to read anything except the same books you had to read when
you were in school." "Yes," her father responded. "When dinosaurs roamed
the earth." "I'm serious, Dad," Mary said. "This is a scandal, and I want
to change it. I've written an editorial for the school newspaper and already
have more than one hundred signatures on my petition to demand that
African American writers become part of required reading for students at
every level." "That's wonderful," her father replied. "I'm sure that the principal will appreciate your passion." And with that, the conversation ended.*

*Mary, true to her word, submitted the editorial, which was published
in the school paper, and took her petition with a growing number of signatures to the school administration. "Very impressive," said Dr. Henson, the
principal. "You know I'm with you on this," he said. A Black Lives Matter
poster was displayed prominently on his wall, and his bookcase was filled to
the brim with African American writers. Mary thought this victory might
be a bit too easy, and then the principal continued. "Mary, this school has a
proud tradition of anti-racism and social justice. These are part of our core
values. But so is academic freedom. Our English teachers have created a*

widely varied reading list representing authors from many cultures and ethnic backgrounds. They encourage students to choose African American literature every year. "Yes, sir," Mary interrupted, "but it's not required. You can get highest honors in this place and never read a single Black author!" Dr. Henson replied, "In almost every conversation I have with students, parents, and teachers, they complain that there is too much to do and not enough time. You're suggesting that we add more required reading to their already overburdened schedules? And if we make this a requirement, will we also include required reading from writers from Native Nations, Pacific Islands, and every other ethnic group? We'll never make everybody happy, and it will never fly with the English faculty. Besides," he said in a misguided attempt at humor, "I don't think your classmates will become very woke by reading CliffsNotes of 'Letter From Birmingham Jail.'" Mary was on the verge of saying something that might get her into trouble, so she just gritted her teeth, gathered her books, and left the office.

> Discussion questions: What should Dr. Henson do? What should the English faculty do? What should Mary and the students who signed the petition do?

Opportunities or Privilege

Mr. Stanford was a leading voice for equity in his school system, facilitating task forces for preK–12 teachers, all of which were designed to create expanded college opportunities for students. He knew the statistics cold: while African American students constituted more than a third of the student population, fewer than 20 percent of gifted and talented classes included African American students, and fewer than 10 percent of AP classes and International Baccalaureate classes in high school included them. Only a fraction of those actually took and passed the AP and IB tests. "The whole selection process is a farce," he said in a task force meeting. "We sort kids at a very early age, and if we don't expect higher performance, especially in nonfiction writing, early in school, then they don't have a prayer on these exams that so heavily emphasize college-level writing. I know that we can do better, and I'd like the task force to recommend that we add writing centers, just like colleges have, at every middle and high school; that we actively recruit more Black and Brown students into advanced classes; and that we have systems in place to help them succeed. And at the elementary level, we need to expand our gifted and talented classes to include everyone—no admission tests required. Let's assume that all of our children are going to college and start that assumption, and the teaching practices that support that assumption, at a very early age."

Mr. Stanford was widely respected in his district and community, and also served as a part-time pastor in the same African Methodist Episcopal church in which he was raised. His classroom walls were covered with posters of Martin Luther King Jr. and other titans of the civil rights movement. He devoted his personal and professional lives to creating greater opportunities for disadvantaged students. Mr. Stanford was surprised when some faculty he saw as allies disapproved of his clarion call for opportunity equity, including a young teacher he mentored. She was the most committed white person he had ever met, someone whose commitment to equity and racial justice never wavered.

"Mr. Stanford," she began, "you know that we love and respect you, but your focuses on AP, International Baccalaureate, and gifted classes all have one thing in common—they are defining success for our students with standards that the white power establishment created. You know that we love you, Mr. Stanford, and we know that you are not in any way a racist, but sometimes it seems that you are advocating for a racist system that is not right for our students." Mr. Stanford was thunderstruck. He had seen students become the first in their families to go to college and graduate. They went on to successful careers, and their letters to him were among his most prized possessions. He read some of those letters aloud to his classes every year. Now he was being told that he was a tool for a racist system? He barely controlled his emotions as he asked, "Are you saying that we should not give our Brown and Black students access to the best opportunities in our educational system? Are you saying," his voice now quivering, "that we should return to past decades in which Black students go to special education and AP classes where there might as well have been a 'whites only' sign on the door? I'm still the chairman of this department, and that's not going to happen on my watch." The next day, Mr. Stanford was scheduled to speak to the Black Student Union at his alma mater. He had intended to use this platform to

encourage more students to go into teaching and school leadership. Now he wasn't so sure what to tell them.

> **Discussion questions: What should Mr. Stanford do? What should his colleagues and school administrators do?**

The Language of Opportunity or Oppression

Mr. Joseph was proud of his position as a fifth-grade teacher. A high school and collegiate debate champion, Mr. Joseph had known he had the hopes of his family riding on his shoulders. Every Thanksgiving dinner included an argument about whether he should go to law school or Wall Street and how everyone knew that he would make his family proud. When he announced his intention to teach, his family assumed this meant he would become a professor. When he said that he intended to teach elementary school in the same urban school system where he was educated, his family tried to show some pride, but their disappointment was evident. Nevertheless, Mr. Joseph persisted and was soon noticed as a star educator in Belmont Elementary, a building that was more than one hundred years old and had been segregated until the 1960s.

Taking a page from his own training, Mr. Joseph not only addressed the typical fifth-grade academic standards but also had his students engage in debate, oratory, extemporaneous speaking, poetry, and declamation—reading great speeches from history with feeling and deep understanding. "We're not going to recite 'I Have a Dream' once a year and call it good," he told his colleagues. "These students are scholars, and I'm going to treat them as such." He insisted that his students use what he called the language of power— Standard English—and he did not permit slang and especially coarse language, including derogatory terms for women and African Americans—in his classroom. "I don't care if it's from your favorite rapper—that language will not be used in my class," he said with authority. Early in the school year, the principal asked to meet with Mr. Joseph, who assumed that he was being asked to lead a committee or take on another task as an emerging faculty leader. Although he was busy meeting the academic and personal needs of his students, he never refused such a request. "What can I do for you?" asked Mr. Joseph. The principal replied, "This is awkward for me, but I've heard some concerns from parents that I wanted to pass along to you. They said that you were censoring their children and limiting their expression. These parents are as committed to social justice as you are, and they feel that your emphasis on traditional rhetorical practices such as debate and declamation are of a different age. One of them is a college professor and has written scholarly articles on how this sort of education perpetuates inequity and reflects a white power structure. He is very emphatic about it and is threatening to take his complaints to the school board. And you know what? After attending the district's anti-racism trainings this year, I think he may be right. As a white person, I was applauding your work because it seemed so comfortable for me, but now I know that it just reflects my white worldview, and that's not what we're about at this school."

"Do you think," Mr. Joseph began slowly, "that students who casually use the N-word and denigrate women with slurs are just part of the culture? Do you think that I should just give them a pass because that's what they hear on the streets? I've got to get these students ready for middle school, high school, and college!" "I understand," said the principal, "but you also have to live in the 21st century where your students are living. And I have to live with the fact that we have very politically active parents who can put our school and me in jeopardy if we don't make some changes." Mr. Joseph left the office wondering if he had made the wrong choice. Was it too late to try law school or Wall Street? Perhaps those professions would appreciate his idea of excellence.

> Discussion questions: What should Mr. Joseph do? What should the principal do?

Conclusion

While teaching and school leadership are among the most personally rewarding jobs on the planet, as our collective experience indicates, they are also exceptionally challenging. Schools are the subject of advice from almost everyone because, after all, most of us went to school and can use our experience as authority. It is not surprising, therefore, that teachers and administrators receive a lot of advice and direction, some of which is contradictory. We are not offering pat answers but rather using the scenarios in this chapter to ask readers—including students and parents—to walk a few steps in the shoes of teachers and administrators. In the next chapter, we consider racial violence and the terrible toll it has taken on communities and families.

CHAPTER 12

Talking About Violence: How Can We Talk About Terrible Things?

George Floyd's murder galvanized, and many would say traumatized, the United States. But does it really take a murder—especially one captured on video for all to see—for white people to get it (Gillard, 2020)? It may have escaped the notice of those wearing their newly minted Black Lives Matter apparel that the movement started not in 2020 but seven years earlier, and efforts like the Black Power movement, Chicano movement, and similar activism even earlier. Before summer 2020 when tearful whites joined the protests, one unarmed Black person after another died in police custody, and many more were injured (Gladwell, 2019). There are helpful tool kits designed for white people to participate in the movement, available at Black Lives Matter's "Resources" (https://black livesmatter.com/resources) page. But surely many readers of this book must be thinking, "Really? Just now this is important? What happened? Oh yes, the United States saw a Black person die on television—again."

When the United States became more deeply mired in the unwinnable Vietnam War, flight after flight delivered young men in body bags to somber funerals and proud parents certain that their sons had died for the just cause of defeating Communism. The tide against the war did not turn in 1968 because the war had suddenly become unjust and unwinnable, but because the sheer futility and brutality of the war were at last brought to living rooms by trusted newscasters. Walter Cronkite, the CBS anchor described as the most trusted man in America, and the man who had announced the death of President John F. Kennedy in 1963, told his audience directly in 1968 that the war was not winnable (Achenbach, 2018). A few months later, President Lyndon Johnson decided not to run for re-election, and Richard Nixon pledged that he would bring the war to an honorable end. We doubt that helicopters fleeing Saigon in 1975 as our Vietnamese allies futilely clung to the struts beneath the aircraft were what most Americans had in mind as an honorable departure. Lie after lie, more than fifty thousand dead Americans, and hundreds of thousands of dead Vietnamese, preceded the conventional wisdom that, of course, we were against the Vietnam War. Exchange the peace sign of the newly aware opponents of the Vietnam War for a Black Power salute and a freshly pressed Black Lives Matter T-shirt, and you have the crowds of the summer of 2020. Were Americans' insights changed, or was it merely that the vivid, visual images of dead people were so obvious, odious, and horrible that those who ignored police brutality and racism no longer could?

Triggers and Truth

According to professor of psychology Nick Haslam (2017), words and images we associate with traumatic events, such as violence, sexual assault, natural disasters, or predatory animals, can spark physical revulsion and post-traumatic stress among those who read those words and view those images. Universities and academic associates have debated the degree to which classes, specific pieces of literature, song lyrics, and other potentially disturbing media should require a trigger warning, but of the following two factors there is little doubt. First, it is difficult to find a great novel, poem, song, myth, opera, or any other piece of literature or music that doesn't contain violence, heartbreak, sex, or other potentially disturbing content. Second, attempts to protect students, and especially teenagers, from these themes are likely to be unsuccessful. The practical implications of this for educators are that on the one hand, we need to have honest and challenging discussions about race and racism. On the other hand, if we attempt to have these conversations without addressing violence and deeply disturbing words, then the conversation is anything but challenging.

Some readers can recall when education about sexual and reproductive health was late, inscrutable, and ineffective. Over time, however, the age at which explicit sex education is first provided to public school students declined, along with the decreasing age for the onset of puberty (da Loba, 2013). Parents can, of course, withhold this information from their children just as they can, we suppose, protect them from the indiscretions of Greek gods, signers of the Declaration of Independence, slave owners, and most U.S. presidents. But the question educators face in the 21st century is, Where is the line between legitimate protection of children who are not ready for complex and disturbing subjects and the essential understandings required for survival in a complex and challenging world?

Scenarios About Change

In this chapter, we explore three scenarios that include explicit inclusion of violence in discussions about race and racism. We are not offering answers but rather suggesting that if we fail to consider these delicate and difficult scenarios now, we will be facing them sooner than we think.

The Last Hours of George Floyd

Allison Simpson has coached the high school drama club for the past five years. In addition to her master's in fine arts, she was an artist in residence at the Globe Theatre in London, where she studied Shakespeare, and she also learned from new wave artists at the world's leading fringe theater festival in Edinburgh, Scotland. Her passion is contagious, and her students readily pick up not only on her commitment to theatrical excellence but also her passion for bringing relevant social awareness to the theater. The drama club has tripled in size under her leadership, with students producing a broad range of plays, including Greek tragedies, Shakespearean comedies, and Broadway shows. She also encourages students to write and produce their own works, and it is one of these efforts that landed Ms. Simpson in the principal's office.

"Please tell me," the principal began, "that you do not have students practicing a play about the last hours of George Floyd." "Of course I do," replied Ms. Simpson. "The students wrote, directed, and rehearsed it. They are hoping to present it to a schoolwide assembly. It's the most talked-about issue in school right now, and theater is a great way to make this tragic event come alive for our students." Principal Silver grabbed her laptop so tightly that Ms. Simpson thought it would break. Principal Silver was a survivor, with sharp political instincts that had allowed her to outlast four superintendents and every other high school principal in this large suburban

district. "*I just got off the phone with a board of education member whose son attends this school.*" *They both knew which student, and most teachers had steered clear of him and his mother, who apparently perceived her role as a school board member to include supervision of everything from algebra tests to cafeteria food. Anything she considered amiss in the school soon became fodder for an inquiry from the board to the superintendent, and those inquiries were soon transmuted into demands that landed on Principal Silver's desk.*

"*Honestly, Allison,*" *Principal Silver began.* "*Graphic violence? The N-word? Choral shouts of 'I can't breathe'? It's all just too much!*" *Ms. Simpson had become accustomed to people mistaking her congenial personality and conspicuous courtesy for weakness.* "*Our students didn't make this up, you know,*" *she replied.* "*Every word in this play came from news reports, which, by the way, they found in our school library. There's nothing nefarious going on here.*" "*You can't do this,*" *Principal Silver replied.* "*I can, and I will,*" *said Ms. Simpson, a bit more stridently than she had intended.* "*These students have worked so hard on this. It's the only way they think they can make a contribution to the Black Lives Matter movement and honor the memory of Mr. Floyd. We can't let this moment in history go by like nothing happened.*" "*Look,*" *Principal Silver said a bit more gently,* "*I understand the passion of youth, but you need to understand the politics of the board. If we produce this play, I will be toast. I had tenure before I became an administrator, so I guess I can go back to my old job in the English department. Perhaps I'll take over the drama club, and we can alternate between* My Fair Lady *and* Oklahoma! *until I retire.*" *She meant it as a small attempt at humor, but Ms. Simpson was not laughing.* "*I don't want you to lose your job either, Principal Silver. But these students are depending on me, and I promised them that the show would go on. Besides, what do you think the Black students, families, and faculty will think when they learn that we failed to teach and learn honestly about Mr. Floyd?*"

Discussion questions: Why does Ms. Simpson believe a play is the way to honor Mr. Floyd's death? What are other teaching resources or alternatives she can use to discuss the reality of racial profiling? What should the principal do? What about the superintendent and the board? What advice do you have for the students and faculty involved with the drama club?

History Without Violence

Mr. Sheffield, a veteran history teacher, prided himself on how he brought history and current events to life in his class. He remained a vibrant and energetic force in the classroom despite his more than forty years as a teacher. He started out of college when he was twenty-one, and now told colleagues that "Sixty is the new thirty" and that he had no intention of hanging up his chalk. This year, he had teamed up with a first-year teacher, Ms. Clark, who loved Mr. Sheffield's enthusiasm and desire to remain relevant to his students. As they studied the history of racism and conflict in the United States, the teachers planned to use film clips of everything from Roots, *depicting the savagery of slavery, to contemporary music, such as Janelle Monáe's "Hell You Talmbout," in which the chorus encourages those singing along to say the names of unarmed people police killed. Most administrators gave Mr. Sheffield a very wide berth, allowing him broad latitude in what to teach and how to teach it. His track record of reaching students who were disengaged in other classes was outstanding, and the feedback from the nearby high school was that the students from Mr. Sheffield's class were almost always the best prepared for the rigors of ninth grade compared to other incoming students.*

But Ms. Clark was another story. As a first-year teacher, her every move, including lesson plans and supporting materials, was scrutinized not only by school-based instructional coaches but also by district curriculum leaders. And in their view, Monáe and any song with the word "hell" in the title were not remotely close to authorized curricula. Mr. Sheffield was livid at the intrusion. He fumed in the principal's office, "We have a hard enough time attracting Black teachers to our profession and, let's be blunt, to this school in particular. Clark is one of the best and brightest I've seen. She could have gone to law school or business school, but here she is, as a first-year social studies teacher doing exceptional work and putting in eighty-hour weeks, and you want me to stifle her?" "It's more than the curriculum," the principal began. "You have a student, Evette Baskin, who suffered the murder of her mother just a few months ago. She needs you, and she needs Ms. Clark. But she doesn't need a daily reminder of violence. Just stick to the history curriculum and find another way for Clark to exercise her creativity." With that, the principal stood up and showed the most committed history teacher in the district out the door.

> Discussion questions: What should
> Mr. Sheffield do? What should he tell Ms. Clark
> and his students? What should the principal
> do? What other supports should the school
> make available to Evette and her family?

Conclusion

In the previous chapters, we considered how to have challenging conversations about race and racism in schools. We know that discussions are the beginning of understanding, and that as understanding deepens, students, teachers, and educational leaders will want to move from discussion to action. That is the subject of the chapters in part 3.

Part 3

Moving From Discussion to Action

And just when we thought the conversations could not become more challenging, we move to the next five chapters and consider how we talk with people we love about racism. It's easy to let our minds wander to the crazy relative at the Thanksgiving dinner table who picks fights, spouts outrageous ideas, and seems to enjoy contention. It's a lot more difficult to consider that we might be, regardless of gender, that crazy relative.

Part 3 concludes with a consideration of how we learn and teach others. Scenarios are a start but hardly an end to the process of using challenging conversations about race and racism to inform our learning, behaviors, policies, and practices.

CHAPTER 13

How Do We Engage Our Communities?

Schools and the communities they serve could potentially develop symbiotic relationships of trust, aspiration, and mutual support. Both schools and communities, however, have to define, cultivate, and consistently enhance and monitor these relationships. School-based personnel and district offices foster supportive environments for minority and majority communities and underprivileged communities when they look to understand these communities culturally and establish plans to cultivate the engagement they seek. Furthermore, schools share a community with other institutions, such as government and civil services, and it is to everyone's advantage to seek and establish a synergistic collaboration. This chapter aims to define and explain community engagement, address the potential role for stakeholders, and develop a plan of action to move from passivity to engagement. It reflects the leadership experience of Washington Collado, who is a veteran leader in Florida and an internationally recognized expert in bilingual education and school improvement.

Defining Parental and Community Engagement

As educators and parents, we can always affirm the importance of parental and community engagement. But how do we define it from our own perspective? What do we (educators) mean by *engagement*? What does it look like? What does it imply for schools, parents, and students? How do we as educators plan to cultivate the engagement we seek from families and communities? Finally, as parents, what does it mean to us?

When families and communities become engaged in schools, involvement may take different forms and be driven by different interests. It is an accepted conclusion that involvement benefits everyone. The following are four degrees of involvement.

1. Are not involved; do not engage in school at all

2. Are individually knowledgeable of their children and know school processes

3. Participate in school organizations

4. Are specifically involved in activities, such as music, sports, academic fairs, and art exhibits

To help schools attain maximum engagement, educators must do a clear assessment of the type of community engagement that takes place in their school. They can study the following levels within their school to improve or establish engagement (Castellano, 2018).

- **Level 1:** Invite families to open house and other school events and seek volunteers, but lack focus, clear communication, or targets.

- **Level 2:** Look to engage the community and invite stakeholders to meet with a more targeted approach and provide language translation, food, or childcare to facilitate participation. Keenly celebrate heritage and language through Black History Month, Hispanic Heritage Month, women's contributions, commemoration of the Holocaust, and so on.

- **Level 3:** Look to train and build capacity in the community to obtain the engagement they seek. Provide teachers and parents electronic access and proper training to monitor students' academic and attendance progress and school activities. Establish proper services in their offices and maintain a multilingual, professional, and friendly atmosphere.

- **Level 4:** Have a more deliberate approach with a parent or community liaison; engage in home visits when necessary; maintain ongoing and active relations with local organizations, including faith-based organizations and local government entities such as first responders, police, and so on. Look to have all stakeholders represented in their organization and school councils. Conduct meetings with various topics of interest to the school and the community served.

In order to engage families, we must invite them and make them feel welcome. This involves introducing the community to the school and the school to the community.

Introducing the Community to the School

The first major step toward community engagement is understanding the community's perception of its involvement in school and, frankly, the school's perception of its community, by asking poignant questions, such as, "How well do we know the community we serve and its interests and makeup?" Generally speaking, many communities, particularly Latinx, may see their role as maintaining a respectful and trusting distance of nonengagement and letting the teachers do their jobs. However, as educators, we would make a big mistake in confusing that trust for disdain. Indeed, communities across the United States know, understand, and value the fact that education is the guarantee for their kids to have a better life.

As schools, it behooves us to learn the community's cultural, religious, family, and social dynamics, as well as how we can harness the trust of families and enhance the role these families can potentially play. It is particularly helpful to cultivate a relationship with local institutions, including media and faith-based organizations, that communicate with these families.

When a school understands the community it serves, it looks to showcase, celebrate, and enhance the community's cultural traditions that are often deeply embedded in its way of life, including artistic expressions, music, history, and religion. When schools allow a space for these families to see their cultural expressions in school events, their trust level increases along with their willingness to engage, thereby decreasing their apprehension and distrust. In other words, their pride in belonging to the school is reaffirmed and generates an overall cultural feeling of *mi casa es su casa* and *mi escuela es su escuela*. To this end, school leaders and educators can develop a map of organizations in the community and seek ways to partner up and engage them, particularly in their areas of focus: families, faith-based organizations, news sources, media organizations, civic organizations, and businesses serving the community. Educators who look to strengthen community engagement know specifically the following institutions and are able to garner their input and support at different times and for different reasons.

- Businesses
- Local governments
- Police and fire departments
- Service organizations
- Veteran clubs
- Professional organizations or individual professionals
- Faith-based organizations
- Civic organizations, such as Lions Club and Rotary Club

Schools are important institutions that are integral parts of the community. When communities create a supportive network and synergistically collaborate, it creates a better outlook for everyone. When schools take time to consider the possibilities of relationships with other community institutions, the potential increases for opportunities to collaborate, address urgent matters, and celebrate momentous occasions.

Introducing the School to the Community

After a school deliberately invests time and energy in understanding the intricacies of the community and its social and economic dynamics, as well as its values, cultures, families, and faith-based interests, it must harness the moment and set the stage to personalize the introduction of the school to its community. In a large measure, schools can control their message. Often, schools have a certain reputation that is largely a personal narrative of individual experiences that become generalized. Schools can use specific ways of introducing themselves and clearly identifying the role they can play to entice community engagement. For instance, when parents understand the dynamics of a school and learn the potential it has for their children, they may pursue higher engagement, even if it is simply to follow the progress of their own child. Schools can host activities, such as academic fairs, celebrations of the arts, and sports, for families to enjoy in order for them to see education in action and their children as part of the action. One of the lessons learned during pandemic-related school closures is that opportunities for family and community engagement have increased. In our own work with schools, we have seen that interactive video opportunities have resulted in greater participation in parent-teacher conferences and even parent engagement at school board meetings.

Moving From Passivity to Engagement in One School

When schools make an analysis of how the communities they serve view them, they must ask, "What reasons have we given families to be proud of their school?" "How have we personalized their experiences?" and, finally, "Have we equipped the community to be savvy consumers of our product?" Different actors in the community may have different interests, so it's important to understand and cultivate them. For instance, sports may attract the interest of some parents, while others may pursue music and the arts.

More than we probably realize, schools are complex organizations. Therefore, when we invest time in cultivating community trust, it sets the tone for understanding the intricacies and complexities of our school systems. For parents, it is sometimes difficult to understand our system of education, as simple as it may seem to us. Besides the complexities, language, culture, and technology, not to mention a complete educationist jargon that educators use rather naturally but that is a foreign language to the communities they serve, can impede engagement.

When a community engages with a school, it has knowledge of the school's operational practices, including school calendars, structure, personnel, and offices. But considering the fact that community engagement relies on trust, it is also imperative that the community knows and understands the safety practices and precautionary measures the school implements for the safety and benefit of students and staff.

Strengthening Students Academically

Many families think school involvement refers to merely assisting children with homework, class projects, and other academic necessities beyond their abilities. Schools can conduct parent training and workshops showing how to support their children in becoming better students. Other ideas for training and workshops can be attendance-improving initiatives, homework tips, and how to help your children maximize the benefits of studying at home. Schools can also look to enhance their parents' engagement with very basic training. They can teach parents how to use technology to follow up on their children's academic progress and how to read report cards, interim progress reports, academic calendars, and exam schedules.

Conclusion

For schools to improve and sustain quality engagement, there must be a plan to attain the quality engagement they seek. These plans of action will showcase how schools will cultivate, foster, celebrate, and take pride in the full integration of the community in their school: academically, socially, culturally, and with a perspective of success in the future through maximizing present potential. When parents are engaged in the education of their children, the students get better grades and are able to have a more positive experience in school. Furthermore, when schools take into account the home language and cultural values of the parents and use bilingual and bicultural approaches to seek effective involvement, the parents' engagement and management of the school's information increase. This engagement represents greater support through accountability for the students. Social-emotional support for the students improves as parents become increasingly engaged, and deeper parental involvement reassures the student and allows the parent to intervene as necessary. Finally, in order to move from increased involvement to engagement, schools must provide parent trainings, encourage open lines of communication, use home language as a communication tool, and cultivate the level of engagement they seek from parents.

With a thoughtful coalition of parents and community support, we can make effective change in schools. Nevertheless, change is profoundly difficult, so in the next chapter, we consider how to transform advocacy into action.

CHAPTER 14

How Can We Advocate for Change?

Change is difficult, and the wait for change can be heart-wrenching. Waiting to hear from the surgeon if your loved one has survived. Waiting to hear if you will receive a scholarship. Waiting to know if your parent has been laid off. And yes, waiting for justice that has eluded previous generations. These changes that require shifts in policy, practice, attitudes, and beliefs can appear to be overwhelmingly difficult. But if the history of racial justice in the United States has taught us anything, it is that change is possible. Martin Luther King Jr. is frequently quoted as saying, "The arc of the moral universe is long, but it bends toward justice." In fact, writes author Mychal Denzel Smith (2018), King was quoting 19th century abolitionist clergyman Theodore Parker, who first uttered the phrase in 1853. Historians differ on the interpretation of King's choice of this quotation. Does it convey hope for justice now, or counsel endless patience for justice in the future? The answer lies perhaps in King's (1964/2010) book *Why We Can't Wait*. Read King's sermons, and the wait could be measured in eons. Read his speeches on nuclear weapons, the Vietnam War, and racial justice, and the wait could be measured in days. But regardless of the context— theological, political, or practical—there is a through line in King's writings on change, and that is it is up to us to make the first move. From individual efforts to the collective actions of students, political groups, and nations, it is action that precedes change. We are not to wait for change to happen in order to legitimize our work.

In this chapter, we will consider the evidence on how change happens, and the answer may surprise you. Change does not happen as a result of stirring oratory or heartfelt workshops that transform the attitudes and beliefs of participants. In fact, this endless appeal for buy-in is a prescription for avoiding change. If individuals and organizations are to change, then we must first change practices, then observe the impact of those practices, and finally, however slowly, attitudes and beliefs will follow. The path toward justice is not, we submit, through a five-year strategic plan, as the cost of delay is too great. The time is now.

We also consider the role of student leadership in change. Late congressperson John Lewis was recognized as an icon for his lifelong activism that began with the civil rights movement, but we dare not forget that he began as a leader of the Student Nonviolent Coordinating Committee and, in his twenties, was the youngest speaker on the dais in Washington, DC, when King told the United States of his dream. We conclude with the most challenging conversation of all—when there is a confrontation between policies and principles.

How Change Happens

Ask your colleagues to put the following elements of the change process in order.

- Change hearts and minds with evidence and arguments.
- Change practices.
- Collect evidence of the impact of change.

If they are familiar with the change literature research since the 1980s, then they will likely respond that these three elements of change are in the right order. After all, wave after wave of change theorists admonish us to create a sense of urgency, build a coalition, and then . . . someday . . . change will happen. This is the theory behind professional learning workshops that are based on bringing in just the right speaker to gain buy-in, then developing a convoluted strategic plan for implementation, and then implementing ever so slowly the changes necessary. Results? That will happen about one year after the expiration of the superintendent's contract. Fortunately, there is an emerging body of evidence on change that shows that traditional models of change have failed (Boyatzis, Smith, & Van Oosten, 2019); that the proper sequence of change is to begin with practices, even before buy-in occurs (Guskey, 2020); and that a new model of change leadership is possible and essential (Reeves, 2021). We are gravely concerned that even with the urgency that the nation and world should clearly have in the aftermath of George Floyd's murder, the focus remains on attitudes rather than policies and practices. Call us cynical, but we have never seen someone who spent thirty or forty years inhaling racist ideas, assumptions, and practices give them up because of a workshop or speech. Yes, they cry the tears of white guilt about the underrepresentation of Black and Latinx students in AP classes, but then fall into old conversations the next day after the tears have dried.

- "You don't really expect them to accept underprepared students in their AP classes, do you?"

- "Yes, we know that students of color dominate the rolls of those receiving Ds and Fs, but we are trying to teach responsibility here, so you really can't tell me that I have to change my grading and reporting systems. I do feel really, really bad about that."

- "Of course, I know that Black and Latinx students are overrepresented in our suspensions and expulsions, but I'm trying to teach social-emotional learning here, and that means setting and reinforcing high standards and expectations for the behavior of all students."

These statements and others like them are redolent of the old racist slur "Give 'em an inch and they'll take a mile."

Of course, none of these people are racists. They are our colleagues and friends. They became teachers and administrators because they want to help students. However, when it comes to change, they find it much easier to "swim in the swamp" of feelings than to "crawl out of the bog" and actually make structural changes. Our collective experience is that when a leader tells us they have buy-in from their staff, then one of two things is true. Either the leader is not asking for any sort of significant change in policy and practice, or the real arguments are happening not in faculty meetings but in the parking lot and on social media. It's hardly a news flash to say that change is difficult. What we offer in the context of challenging conversations about race and racism is that we can actually do something about it. We do not need to settle for another decade or two of whining rhetoric that leads nowhere. We want to make change happen now.

The Cost of Delay

What is the cost if we fail to rise to the occasion? The cost in lives is compelling enough for some parents and community groups. But policy makers often want hard data, so here we go. The return on investment for quality early childhood care is greater than three to one, one of the best returns of any governmental expenditure (Kristof & WuDunn, 2019). But the greatest return by far of any social investment is the cold-hearted calculations in avoiding high school dropouts. The Alliance for Excellent Education (https://All4Ed.org) has created calculations for every state, and it considers both the expense of dropouts in terms of additional expenses for health care and the criminal justice system and the lost revenues from the income, property, and sales taxes that high school graduates pay—far greater than their peers who failed to finish.

The impact that we make does not have to be huge. Just a 1 percent improvement in the high school graduation rate in Nebraska—1 percent!—results in $1.3 million savings on health care, a $4.7 million gain in home sales, and $380,000 more in federal tax revenue, and that's a pretty good start. We have not begun to address the human toll taken in intergenerational poverty that high school failure fuels and, conversely, the long-term success of intervention. One does not need, in brief, rhetoric about structural racism and its consequences. Taking steps to reduce inequities in education results directly in fewer failures by all students, and because Black and Latinx students fail in disproportionate numbers, reducing their failure rate helps not only them but everyone in the community. This confirms the biblical observation that it rains on the just and unjust (Matthew 5:45, Revised Standard Version), meaning that even the biggest opponent of racial equity in your community will enjoy the benefits of improved revenues, lowered expenses, and a stronger employment base. This evidence is so overwhelmingly compelling that opposition to it speaks volumes about why getting buy-in is futile. People who oppose equity are literally unable to support their own self-interest if it means abandoning previously held positions. So, in the new model of change, we are not asking them to change their previously held positions—we are simply asking them to do it. We are, to put a fine point on it, not asking faculty members, administrators, or parents to buy into effective feedback, grading, and reporting practices.

We are rather suggesting that educators implement these policies because they are in the best interests of the entire community, not because they are popular.

The Role of Student Leadership in Change

In chapter 10, we acknowledged the tendency of well-intentioned leaders and policy makers to engage in the hero complex, in which they swoop in and save the poor children from their calamity. This is the "fixer" mentality that is the opposite of the *multiplier*, who, according to researcher Liz Wiseman (2017), empowers students and communities to make the change rather than merely be the recipients of change. Therefore, change leaders are wise to engage the passion, courage, and commitment of students. As writers, speakers, and consultants, we wish we could say that we were the authors of successful change, but we encourage readers to beware of anyone making such a claim. Our job is to empower the change agents in your classrooms and faculty rooms to make the case for change to your community and policy makers. For example, when it comes to dismantling structures that led to indefensible failure rates for Black and Latinx students, we have seen teacher leadership be effective from coast to coast, from small systems to large ones. While we all believe in evidence on a national and global scale, we know from experience that the best evidence to support change is what comes from your own community. That inside-out model of change removes all the barriers. When advocates say, "We know that this works because we've done it—with our schedule, without a budget, and with our union bargaining agreement. Please don't tell us how impossible it is and how it's going to take five years to make a change." Students are especially compelling when it comes to developing a sense of urgency, because it's very difficult to tell an eight-year-old in a school where students are struggling to read that you have a real swell five-year plan for them. High school sophomores, whose time horizon is sometimes measured in moments, are similarly impatient with the typical plans and processes of adults who seem mired in the Paleolithic tar sands that adolescents assume is our natural habitat.

In sum, students of all faiths and none instinctively follow the words of the sage Rabbi Hillel (as cited in Landsberg, 2013), who reminds us all, "If not now, when?"

Principles Before Policies

We recognize that our passion for equity and our frustration with the slow pace of change can reveal an impatience that is counterproductive. Therefore, we wish to conclude this chapter with a technique that we have found useful in accelerating the pace of change and bringing divergent interest groups together. This is the concept of *principles before policies*. It is exceptionally difficult for a conversation with faculty, parents, and other interest groups to go anywhere if we begin in the weeds of policies. Partisans on all sides routinely defend their policy turf, explaining that their policy is divinely inspired and the policies of their opponents are the instruments of the underworld. So, let us back away from the metaphorical boxing ring and ask not who has the better debating points for one policy or another but rather where can we find common ground. For example, two principles on which even the most divergent groups can agree include accuracy and fairness. Accuracy can seem so obvious that it may not be worth pointing out, but it shifts the entire tenor of a conversation when we change an insight from "this policy contributes to structural racism"—however true that might be—to a statement that "this policy is inaccurate; it's just a math error." That takes the emotional charge right out of the discussion. Rather than sputtering about "the way Mrs. Spence taught me was good enough then, and it's good enough now" or "alleging that my system is racist is a personal insult," let's change the conversation. The debates in the late 20th century about the bell curve (Herrnstein & Murray, 1996) ranged from a thoughtful discourse on the nature of data and their implications for policy to cavalier allegations of racism over the tables that showed evidence that, among other things, Black students scored lower on tests, performed poorly in school compared to their white counterparts, and had lower lifetime earnings. Assuming that the reader was willing to slog through more than nine hundred pages and was familiar with these data sources, this was simply true. It didn't make the authors guilty of racism any more than the economists and sociologists who gather these data in the first place were Klansmen. Data have no more point of view than does gravity, the rotation of the earth, or the relationship between the sides of a triangle. How we interpret these data and what we do about them, by contrast, are clearly a matter of principle.

If we say, "The bell curve is morally bankrupt, and its advocates are guilty of bias," then we are unlikely to have an illuminating conversation. If by contrast, as Doug and his colleague argue (Reeves, 2007), it was not necessary to challenge the integrity or racial animus of the authors of the bell curve in order to challenge their application of the normal distribution of student performance, we could start a constructive conversation. Moreover, we did not simply say that the bell curve was awful, leaving policy makers and educators with no alternative. Rather, we offered a superior alternative—the mountain curve—that showed that while there are certainly differences among students, many of those differences have to do with factors outside our assessment objectives.

Similarly, we need not question the motives and integrity of those who cling to inaccurate student assessment, reporting, and feedback systems because those systems are part of long-held policies of racial inequity. Rather, we can and should challenge the mathematics. Teachers in San Bernardino, California, and Cleveland Heights, Ohio, for example, brought to their board their proposals for improved feedback systems not by calling the previous policies racist—though the racial inequities were obvious for all to see. Rather, they simply said, "Because we all share a commitment to accuracy, we propose that feedback and reporting systems remove mathematical inaccuracies." This included, for example, removing interval errors (the interval between a D and F was six times greater than the interval between a D and a C—an obvious miscalculation). Similarly, the teachers challenged descriptive mathematics errors, such as the arithmetic mean. The mean, or average, is only one statistic to describe performance, and as our scenarios about student athletics suggest, the average is simply inaccurate. Teachers achieved an immediate result, in a single semester, reducing the failure rate for students who were predominately Black and Hispanic by more than 80 percent. We have seen similar results from the farm country of Iowa to densely populated urban areas. When we agree on principles such as accuracy and fairness, we can remain focused on what is most important—improving equity and opportunity for students and avoiding unnecessary and diversionary arguments over the motives of people with whom we disagree. As we said at the outset, our objective is not to change hearts and minds. Rather, our objective is to change policy and practice, and to do so right now.

Conclusion

We are pragmatists and know well the frailties of argument and evidence, no matter how well reasoned. We would have happily wagered our collective dinners on the fact that we persuaded a board or community to join the fight, only to find that backroom deal making doomed what seemed like an obvious win. Our purpose is not to whine about it but to deal with disappointment and loss in a straightforward manner, as these losses help us and the schools we serve prepare to fight another day. That is the subject of our next chapter.

CHAPTER 15

Why Isn't Being Right Enough?

We have all served playground duty in our careers and heard the plaintive cry, "That's not fair!" While we brush away tears, soothe hurt feelings, and try to resolve playground conflicts, we stifle the inner voice that says, "Better get used to it, kid. Life is not fair." We should not, however, succumb to cynicism, not only because it is a terrible model for students but also because cynics do not last in the profession of education. But one does not have to be a cynic to recognize that disappointment and loss are real. There is an enormous gap between what we know to be just, right, and good and the reality that our students and their families face every day. In this chapter, we recognize that disappointment, and the stress and anxiety that accompany it, can be debilitating, and we offer practical steps to provide the resilience needed to survive.

How Disappointment Can Become Debilitating

During the memorial services and remembrances for the late congressperson John Lewis, one scene recurred across television screens. It was when the young Lewis, many years from becoming a congressperson, attempted to engage in peaceful protests and was savagely beaten by officers and civilians alike. While commentators lauded his courage and commitment to nonviolence, they missed an important point. Lewis suffered multiple skull fractures, which are associated with traumatic brain injury that leads to lifelong impairments (King, Finnin, & Kramer, 2018). It doesn't just take a police baton to inflict lasting damage. Disappointment and loss, particularly when powers over which we have no control inflict them, can have both psychological and physical impacts. The damage from continued stress, anxiety, and depression takes a physical toll. Indeed, some freedom riders of the civil rights movement went on to have lifelong traumas, like depression (Blake, 2004). While people in the helping professions such as education, social work, and medical care sometimes like to claim that they can compartmentalize their lives and work through the stress associated with their jobs, the reports from nurses, teachers, physicians, and educational leaders suggest an entirely different reality. Research from the Mayo Clinic confirms that stress is related to headaches, muscle tension or aches, chest pain, fatigue, change in sex drive, upset stomach, and sleep problems (Mayo Clinic Staff, 2019). In a clinical study, anxiety was associated with heart disease, depression, asthma, persistent cough, hypertension, and gastrointestinal problems (Kang et al., 2017). Fortunately, research sheds light not only on the debilitating impacts of stress, anxiety, and depression but also on ways to foster resilience.

In spring 2020, during the COVID-19 pandemic, health-care workers faced what Harvard Medical School researcher Marwa Saleh (2020) calls "stabbing a fresh wound." Not only were they taking on an extra workload with patients testing the capacity of hospitals but also health-care workers were becoming ill themselves, reducing the professional staff available to support increasing quantities of patients with progressively severe ailments. Moreover, physicians had to make heartrending decisions about who would and would not receive lifesaving treatments. China was several months ahead of the United States in facing these challenges, and their medical providers report that 50.4 percent had symptoms of depression, 34 percent report insomnia, 44.6 percent report symptoms of anxiety, and 71.5 percent report distress (Saleh, 2020).

Similarly, teachers and school administrators faced exceptionally stressful conditions during the pandemic. Surveys reveal that teacher morale declined dramatically and that the emotional toll taken not only by the students they see but also especially by the students with whom they are not in contact is devastating (Gewertz, 2020). Not only do simple tasks take longer in a virtual environment but the individual attention on which students depend is sorely lacking in it, even in those cases where students have access to computers and internet connectivity. In some cases, teachers attempted to reach students with individual phone calls and personal visits to homes, speaking to students from sidewalks and driveways. In addition to emotional stress, teachers exhibited physical symptoms of burnout, not surprising from their workdays that extended from the early-morning hours until late at night. Although a good deal of this stress is due to the care that teachers, paraprofessionals, and administrators extend to their students, with more than 92 percent of COVID-19 deaths affecting those age fifty-five and over, and almost 30 percent of the teaching population over age fifty, concerns for personal health also contribute to teacher anxiety.

In order to bounce back from stress, professionals in education (Israel, 2015) and medicine (Saleh, 2020) receive strikingly similar advice. While not all these suggestions work for everyone, at least one or two ideas might be worthwhile for readers who need to have a systematic and thoughtful way to cope.

Resilience in the Face of Disappointment and Loss

Although *resilience* is commonly used to describe the emotional strength to rebound from disappointment and failure, the word actually stems from metallurgy. The origin holds important clues for our consideration of individual and organizational resilience. Almost all materials have some degree of elasticity. This is true even of steel beams that form the foundation of one-hundred-story buildings. If these apparently solid and unbendable beams did not have some elasticity, then at the first shift in the ground—such as that associated with an earthquake—the beams would break apart and the building would come crashing down. If, on the other hand, the beams were too elastic, they would bend so far that the building would fall over. The challenge for structural engineers is to determine the "modulus of resilience" (Dipto, n.d.)—the point at which a metal can bend and then return to its original shape. People and organizations, like steel beams, have their own modulus of resilience. If they are unable to bend at all, they will fall apart under stress. If they bend too much, they can no longer support the emotional loads they carry and are unable to return to their originally strong condition. In the following pages, we will first consider physical resilience, how our bodies can sustain damage and nevertheless bounce back from injury. We then consider emotional resilience and how loss, despair, loneliness, and other emotional injuries can be devastating and yet survivable. Then there is organizational resilience. Just like the human body, organizations can suffer diminished resilience with age. However, just as with physical and emotional resilience, organizations can also bounce back, healing from the disruption of challenge and change.

Consider the following ways to build resilience from the Cognitive Behavior Therapy Center (Johnson, 2020). First, it is important to connect with others, forming healthy relationships with family, friends, and colleagues. This is difficult, but not impossible, to accomplish in a virtual environment. The key is that these are not utilitarian exchanges. You are not saying, "I'd like to get involved with you because it will help me be resilient." Rather, you are seeking connections because you are genuinely interested in other people and their causes, passions, and beliefs. Second, self-care is essential. In education, we tend to valorize the heroic teachers and leaders who "burn themselves to a cinder" in the service of their students. But heroism and the fatigue that inevitably follow repeated extraordinary exertion are not sustainable strategies, and the burned-out teacher and leader cannot help the students and schools they seek to serve. Self-care includes not only nutrition, exercise, and enjoyment but also judiciously turning off phones and other electronic connections in order to have uninterrupted time for contemplation and meditation. Third, there are strong links between regular progress toward meaningful goals and positive intrapersonal and interpersonal relationships. This is what researchers Teresa M. Amabile and Steven J. Kramer (2011) call the *progress principle*. Small daily wins like the page of the manuscript, the single conversation with a colleague, and the kind and unexpected gesture of a friend are the small things that create large quantities of resilience.

The Philosophy of Nietzsche

When the 19th century German philosopher Friedrich Nietzsche (as cited in Stoner, 2019) wrote, "That which does not kill us makes us stronger," he didn't anticipate 21st century researchers who suggest that he was right would fact-check him. Their studies consider the impact of early career failures by academics, and find that, statistically at least, early failure is associated with later success (Stoner, 2019). This is not, we suggest, associated with the failures themselves, but rather with the fact that successful academics tend to publish more, and in order to publish more, they submit more, and as a result of submitting more work to publishers, they receive more rejections. It's a classic logical error, attributing results to one cause that are more accurately attributed to other causes. But headlines like "Nietzsche was right!" are a bit catchier than "News flash: Life is multivariate and somewhat complicated."

Late German philosophers are hard to argue with because, for one thing, they are dead. But that's another logical fallacy—just because a phrase sounds more erudite with the distance of time and geography or, for that matter, if it's expressed in Latin or recited with a British accent, doesn't necessarily make it true. As Ken Williams has pointed out, the Protestant work ethic is appealing on many grounds, including our appreciation for hard work and personal responsibility. But it is only a small leap from the benefits of the Protestant ethic—hard work and persistence are rewarded, and those rewards are therefore deserved—to the converse belief that when bad things happen, like poverty, illness, and illiteracy, they are the result of inadequate work and responsibility. This leads to our justification in the United States, year after year, century after century, of the deep inequities that prevail among the races. It is as if, as Mike Mattos (personal communication, July 26, 2020) has argued, skin pigmentation is somehow related to intelligence and academic potential. When Mattos says that, it jars his listeners because it is so blatant and abrupt. Nevertheless, just because overt racism is disturbing does not mean that subtle racism is any more acceptable.

A more thoughtful analysis of the Nietzsche quotation is that when people survive trauma, it is in spite of the trauma, not because of it. Psychological studies reveal that traumatized children are more, not less, likely to be traumatized again (Shpancer, 2010). Children who are raised in tough neighborhoods become weaker, not stronger, and they are more, not less, likely to struggle in the world. The disappointments that we face and, most important, that our children face are the result not of some bizarre Nietzschean social experiment but rather of our continued tolerance of racist practices and policies. So, what are we to do with this upwelling of disappointment, frustration, hurt, and anger?

As you discuss this book with your students and colleagues and in your community, we hope that you will transform the collective disappointment, frustration, and anger into challenging but productive discussions. Most of all, we hope these discussions lead to policies and practices that will help our schools and the students we serve. We have not offered any solutions for racial tension or racism. Rather, we offer an open door for the challenging and necessary discussions that we all must have with one another.

Conclusion

In this chapter, we have not sought to justify the conditions that lead to disappointment; rather, we have suggested that preparing our students for rejection and disappointment is part of teaching them resilience. The heroes we have used as models almost always have the commonalities of meeting great obstacles, overcoming barriers, persevering through disappointment and loss, and eventually succeeding. It is precisely these character traits of perseverance and resilience that will help our students and colleagues move from advancing racial justice to practicing active anti-racism.

CHAPTER 16

How Do We Create Equity Consciousness?

Yvette Jackson encourages us to begin the journey of creating equity consciousness with practices that elicit the strengths of each student and teacher. Rather than forming prejudgments based on previous records, scores, and observations, she argues we must begin with strengths. The research on strengths-based teaching and leadership is consistent and transnational (Rath & Conchie, 2008), yet the default in many schools is to focus on deficits associated with student characteristics that are most easy to observe—poverty, race, and accent (Kendi, 2020; Kinzler, 2020). In employment, race and gender are protected classes, against which discrimination is illegal. Astonishingly, discrimination based on accent remains legal and rampant. It is not only fashionable to declare that diversity is an asset—it is a reality, this fact established by research about creativity, decision making, and leadership effectiveness. Yet, despite this, many children learn at a very young age to fear those who are different from themselves. It seems obvious, for example, that in the 21st century, children and adults with multilingual capabilities have an advantage. Many seemingly enlightened parents talk about the benefits of multilingual environments but may be unwilling to allow their children to play with children whose linguistic heritage is different (Chugh, 2018). That is why equity consciousness is necessary. It is not enough to mouth kind words about differences; instead, we must consciously embrace those differences. In this chapter, we take a closer look at reciprocity, the differences between culture and race, what it means to listen to students, and what equity consciousness looks like in the classroom.

Understanding Reciprocity

At the core of valuing the strengths of others is understanding reciprocity. If we are to connect with any degree of meaning, we must bring our own frames of reference to a relentless search for affiliation with others. We must teach our children and students to do the same. Infants and adolescents alike are sensitive to affirmation, sensing the warm feelings associated with similarities and the dangers associated with differences. Contrary to their claims, teenagers dye their hair purple not really to be different but rather to fit in with their peers who, in one way or another, wish to distance themselves from their parents. While the authors of this book are not endorsing one hairstyle over another, as the parents of many adolescents, we can't help but note that part of a healthy adolescence is the establishment of growing degrees of independence. Indeed, hair colors not found in nature, along with piercings and torn garments, are not bad ways for adults and peers to resist the temptation to elevate the externalities of appearance over the internal qualities of kindness, empathy, inquisitiveness, and generosity that we can nurture only if we get beyond appearances. As the research on mindset (Dweck, 2016) reminds us, educators err gravely when they praise students for being *smart* (read: being good, conforming, and not taking the time of adults) rather than for the less comfortable behavior of learning through trial, error, exploration, and hard work. Noticing individual efforts and encouraging the growth mindset associated with them requires us to look beyond externalities. These same dynamics play out among adults in interviews for teaching jobs and promotions. When the interviewer thinks that high praise is saying something like, "She reminds me so much of myself!" the school might as well put out a sign that says, "Please take your diversity somewhere else."

Distinguishing Culture From Race

Earlier in the book (in chapter 1, page 15), we note the uncomfortable discussion surrounding the question, "Why is everything about race?" The truth is that many issues in schools, societies, and simple walks down the block with our families are, in fact, often about race. But race and culture are not the same, and we conflate the two at our peril. Culture is what is meaningful and relevant to our students. As educators and leaders, we make a conscious effort to value culture and make pedagogical connections. This is dramatically different from some of the facile claims of cultural relevance in placing a Brown face on a terrible textbook and claiming that underlying prejudices have been transformed. When cultural relevance is commercialized, we are once again imposing one set of backgrounds and conceptual understanding on students and displacing another. Cultural understanding is not about elevating one culture or practice ("Are All Cultures," 1998) but rather about deepening understanding of cultures. That those understandings can lead to feelings of pride, embarrassment, and confusion is precisely what critical thinking is about, and it is the opposite of cultural studies as indoctrination to one point of view or another. Culture is not a *Black thing* but rather the means by which we find relevance in behaviors, traditions, and activities. Our job is not to promote or demote culture but to help students explore culture and the impact it has on our lives today.

Culture influences even seemingly benign exchanges between students and teachers. In Doug's many years of work in Zambia, he saw teachers and administrators bring together members from this nation with seven official languages and deep historical divides by opening ceremonies in which, for example, a Bemba man might gently tease someone from the Copperbelt. But humor designed to defuse generations of antagonism in one cultural context would be regarded as deeply inappropriate ethnic humor in another context. Similarly, Yvette notes that when adults in the same school use sarcasm, they might think it is funny, but to the ears of a student, it can be deeply wounding.

Listening—Beyond Surveys

Teachers and educational administrators are exhausted by surveys, impatient with the time they take, and skeptical of the confidentiality they promise. If we want students to have voice and agency, a standardized survey is little better than the typical standardized test. Students must be part of the design and planning of methods used to seek their views just as they must be part of unit planning in the academic curriculum. Yvette, along with Howard Gardner (1999), is a stickler for high standards. Gardner, who pioneered the theory of multiple intelligences, bristles when he is aligned with forces against high academic standards.

Like Yvette, he advocates for academic rigor, provided rigor is expressed and assessed in a variety of different ways. These two scholars further agree that teachers, not testing companies, define what rigor and high expectations really mean for all students. Genuine listening requires the consideration of students who may look alike but have dramatically different perspectives. The assumption that one Black student speaks for all her African American counterparts is as offensive as assuming that one student from a southern rural background represents every other student who looks or sounds similar.

Ensuring Equity Consciousness in the Classroom

In order to understand what equity consciousness is, we must consider what it is not. For example, Yvette explains that evidence of a failure of equity consciousness is when curriculum is presented without context and without frames of reference relevant to the student. This is the pedagogical equivalent of explaining the Civil War to students by asking them to view *Gone With the Wind*, with a particular focus on the psychodrama between Scarlett and Rhett. Wait, what? Were there other people in that movie? A topic-driven curriculum, the norm in many schools, is about delivery, not understanding, with little or no concern about what students take away—intellectually and emotionally—from the lesson. Yvette cringes when she hears the words, "I created the test, and it's their job to finish it." The profound misunderstanding of rigor is reflected in the phrase, "I know I have high standards, because 60 percent of students failed. If they didn't pass, it's their fault." To be absolutely clear, Yvette does not justify indifference by students—nor does she justify poor study habits or intellectual disengagement. But engagement is not merely the job of the student but the result of a collaborative effort of teachers and students who make social, emotional, and intellectual connections in every lesson. Above all, equity consciousness is not merely about the content of the curriculum but about the interpersonal dynamics of the entire class. When all students are valued and appreciated for who they are as humans, not merely for what they knew before the school year started or how they scored on a test, then we glimpse the beginning of equity consciousness. The imperative of deep listening to students will change the narrative of the classroom from a pedagogy of transmission to the pedagogy of transformation.

Conclusion

In this chapter, we discussed the means by which we can establish equity consciousness—by assiduously embracing people's differences. We must rethink our frames of reference as we seek to make meaningful connections with others, and recognize when our or others' definitions of relatability begin and end with externalities. We forge real connections when we appreciate the strengths in our differences and practice deep listening, challenging any assumptions that students who may look or sound similar share the same experiences and perspectives. In our next chapter, we consider the advice of Anthony Muhammad for next steps and for how to move from learning and listening to taking action.

CHAPTER 17

The Next Chapter: How Do We Shift From Opposing Bigotry to Practicing Anti-Racism?

One should never confuse Anthony Muhammad's easy manner, civility, and thoughtful scholarship with a lack of passion. While he can reach people with differing perspectives with his respectful allowance for different interpretations of events and words, he is crystal clear about the distinction between the avoidance of overt bigotry and the acceptance of subtle racism. It is possible, for example, to have perfect table manners while allowing racial slurs in less time than it takes to say, "Please pass the salt." Therefore, while obvious bigotry has been expunged from many, but not all, schools and from most of polite society, there remains widespread tolerance of racist practices and language. It is not, in brief, the obvious bigots that are the only problem. It is the "polite" racists who talk a good game decrying bigotry while tolerating racism at a deep and continuous level. The thesis of this chapter and of the entire book is that understanding racism is only a first step. If we are to fulfill the promise of a just and equitable society, then we must move from avoiding bigotry to actively opposing racism.

Bigotry and Racism—The Essential Difference

Racism and bigotry are different. *Bigotry* is about crass descriptions of the other: African American children are born to jump high and play basketball (code for "not so great in school"), while Jewish children excel at mathematics (code for "cutthroat financiers"), and Asian children are natural scientists (code for "mysterious and sneaky"). These stereotypes abound, and they are easy to identify and oppose. Less obvious, Anthony points out, are the subtleties of ingrained racism that are part of conversations from the classroom to the boardroom. The greatest challenge as we address racism is that it is easy to identify and call out bigotry, as statements such as "Mexicans are rapists" draw almost universal condemnation. But *subtle* racism? That is where the excuses begin and the learning often stops. If we are to extend our work beyond opposing bigotry to actively opposing racism, the work begins with a willingness to learn.

Words Matter—How Language Shapes Understanding

Doug is very proud of the "world champion" Boston Red Sox, Boston Celtics, New England Patriots, Boston Bruins, and Harvard Crimson. Well, four out of five is not bad. But Anthony explains that there are very few ice hockey teams in Africa, and almost no professional baseball teams in Europe. Moreover, when Doug uses the term *football*, he might consider that the oldest form of the game comes from Australia and that the vast majority of the world regards football as a game played with a spherical ball that would seem out of place on the typical U.S. field of play. The examples may seem trivial, Anthony explains, but every time an American casually uses the term *football*, it grates on the nerves of the 7.2 billion people who do not occupy the United States. It is really not about sports but rather about the casual indifference to our neighbors around the globe.

Racism is socialized, Anthony explains. It is learned and often not deliberate. Therefore, it requires conscious effort to unlearn it. We casually refer to the "World Wars" without acknowledging that there were significant parts of the world that were not at war in 1914 or 1939. These commonly used terms in 21st century textbooks retain the language and perspective that anything outside of Europe and North America is historically and linguistically irrelevant.

Consider the more serious example of handshaking, something that people take for granted as a method of social interaction. But this act, which may feel common particularly for men in North America, was inconsiderate and rude when extended to women in Orthodox Jewish and many Islamic communities in the past. Today, handshaking is potentially life-threatening when extended to anyone in the world because of COVID-19. But even with all the pervasive health warnings, it requires conscious effort to avoid shaking hands when greeting a stranger. Casual racism extends to professional environments as well. We know of African American physicians whose new patients, when the doctors enter a room, direct them to the trash receptacles, with the casual assumption of everyone around them that they are maintenance workers rather than surgeons with sixteen years of postgraduate education.

Even in educational settings that seem dedicated to equity and whose members claim to be anti-racist, we see the assignment of the most talented Black educators and leaders to schools where the student body matches the ethnicity of the prospective teachers and administrators. However well-intentioned these assignments may be, they are redolent of the treatment of Joseph Louis Barrow, a name white promoters changed to "Joe Louis" and who was advertised as "a credit to his race" in the 1930s (National Museum of African American History and Culture, n.d.). This is not equity, but racism, pure and simple. It is the presumption that the skin color of a person defines who he or she is and what he or she means to other people. For all the hand-wringing about the shortage of African American teachers and leaders, it is not a puzzle of Byzantine complexity, to use yet another ethnic stereotype (Why not Aztec complexity—or Ibo, Bemba, or a thousand other traditions known for complicated puzzles?), that when we make working conditions, respect, and safety elusive, we are unlikely to attract the next generation of Black graduates to join our profession.

Practical Anti-Racism

The writers of this book are deeply committed not only to the principle of anti-racism but also to the practical reality that we must move from theory to practice. In order to embrace what Anthony calls *practical anti-racism*, we must begin with an acknowledgment that however much we may avoid bigotry, many middle-class people reading this book benefit from racism. We persuaded ourselves that Black people did not choose to live next to white people rather than consider the practical impact of redlining. Well into the 21st century, racial differences in educational opportunities lead to differences in colleges, jobs, earning power, and, as the cycle repeats itself, housing. While few people actively choose racism, many of us passively accept its benefits.

Consider *redlining*, the practice that systematically excluded Black loan applicants from mortgages in neighborhoods, mortgages for which they were qualified as a result of income, employment, and every conceivable criterion except one—their skin color. The same phenomenon has been established well into the 21st century in studies that compared rental applications by phone with people with identical credit, income, and employment, with the application with Black dialect or distinctively African American names rejected in comparison to the appliances with Doug's flat midwestern twang, and the name of *Douglas* rather than *Denesha*. Almost every person on U.S. soil has benefited from some sort of racism, from the confiscation of the lands of indigenous people to the use of electronics, cars, and clothing that were the product of forced or low-wage labor.

What is the response of the practical anti-racist? We insist that for people like Doug to feel bad, however well intentioned, is an empty gesture. However meritorious street protests might be, practical anti-racism calls on all of us to notice the everyday racism all around us. When a house or apartment near us comes on the market, and we see five prospective buyers or renters, all of whom are white, then we are complicit in the racism if we do not confront the rental or sales agent about this apparently exclusionary listing. In schools, when we see that the same infractions, such as disrespect or disruption, are dealt with in class for most white students and result in office referrals for most Black students, then we must address this forcefully. If we as teachers see two students with the same reading difficulty, and the teacher refers the Black student to special education and his white peer remains in the regular education classroom, then we must call it out. When the Black student fails a high school class for missing homework, never mind the evening job, sibling care, and food insecurity, and the white student under similar circumstances with missing work receives tutoring, then we must name this disparity for what it is. Think of it this way: if you saw a child of any race in front of a moving bus, you would grasp that child out of harm's way. That is precisely the sense of urgency that every teacher, leader, parent, and community member needs when we see a child in front of the racist bus of inequitable discipline, grading, and graduation policies.

Let us be very specific. The path to opportunities for college and all the economic and life opportunities that it provides starts very early. When Anthony began his tenure as a middle school principal, only 7 percent of students were on the path to advanced classes that might open the door to college. Just a few years later, 100 percent of his students, all in a school composed of Black and poor students, were on the track to college. The students did not change parents. They did not change addresses. They did not change skin color. And they did not win the lottery—except with their principal, who set them on the trajectory toward success.

Conclusion

While this is the last chapter in our book, we trust it will be the next chapter in the response of our readers to racism. While we know we cannot change attitudes and beliefs that were engrained over decades and inherited over centuries, we are equally certain of what we can influence, right now—today. We can influence practice and policy. Please do not wait for buy-in. Please do not wait for attitudes and beliefs to change. And to be blunt, anyone who tells you that they can change attitudes and beliefs in a three-hour workshop is mistaken. We are, above all, practical and focused on the needs of our students and children *today*. Therefore, we are committed to the impact that we make right now, today, on students and their opportunities for the future. We leave you four specific and practical actions that every educator, leader, parent, community member, and student can do *right now*.

1. **Assess the assessments:** If Doug, middle school mathematics teacher at heart, were to use story problems about hockey pucks in Zambia, it would be ludicrous. But when our textbooks and state assessments use vocabulary and contexts that exclude students because of their cultural backgrounds, then it's not a joke. It's racist. And we have an obligation to call it out. Therefore, let's examine every test question on the basis of the classic psychometric criteria of validity and reliability. *Validity* is, simply put, the assertion that we are testing what we think we are testing. Therefore, the question we must all ask is, "Are we really assessing mathematics, science, or literacy, or are we assessing cultural, linguistic, or ethnic background?"

2. **Challenge your friends:** Doug is earnest about this subject, and probably too much so sometimes. Ken Williams chided Doug by saying, "OK, OK, you can put on your 'I'm not a racist' badge today." If you are lucky enough to have a friend like Ken, then you can accept that challenge, even if it stings a little. Honest conversation requires honest challenges. And friendships are only as good as their ability to withstand challenges. Doug would admit that he has, in the words of Robert Frost, "miles to go before I sleep" (Poetry Foundation, n.d.). And Ken would counter with the words of Maya Angelou, "If you are always trying to be normal, you will never know how amazing you can be" (Farnam Street, n.d.).

3. **Stop saying, "I'm not a bigot":** Let's just stipulate that if you have read our book this far, we acknowledge that you are not a bigot. But as Anthony contends, there are explicit differences between bigotry and racism. We can reject the former and simultaneously benefit from the latter. The more insightful statement is not against bigotry, an unchallenging target. Rather, say something that is hard. Even though I don't feel like a racist, I have certainly benefited from racism, from the home into which I was born, the schools I attended, the jobs I received, and the daily benefits—food, shelter, medical care, and law enforcement—that I take for granted.

4. **Give one another grace:** Anthony can reduce an audience to a puddle of tears, full of contrition and regret. Then, he surprises them with the following recollection. When he was running track, his coach told him, "You'd better not lose to that white boy." And Anthony did not. He had a mindset of superiority. Moreover, his competitors had defeated themselves, Anthony noted, because they thought "Black men are faster than me." Anthony concludes, "We're not bad people. We are just socialized that way."

We have written the last chapter. We now challenge you to write the next chapter.

References and Resources

Achenbach, J. (2018, May 25). Did the news media, led by Walter Cronkite, lose the war in Vietnam? *The Washington Post.* Accessed at www.washingtonpost.com/national/did-the-news-media-led-by-walter-cronkite-lose-the-war-in-vietnam/2018/05/25/a5b3e098-495e-11e8-827e-190efaf1f1ee_story.html on July 26, 2020.

Advocacy. (n.d.). In *Merriam-Webster's online dictionary.* Accessed at www.merriam-webster.com/dictionary/advocacy on January 28, 2021.

Amabile, T. M., & Kramer, S. J. (2011). The power of small wins. *Harvard Business Review, 89*(5), 70–81.

Are all cultures equal? (1998). Accessed at http://archive.wilsonquarterly.com/in-essence/are-all-cultures-equal on July 29, 2020.

Bergner, D. (2020, July 15). "White fragility" is everywhere. But does antiracism training work? *The New York Times.* Accessed at www.nytimes.com/2020/07/15/magazine/white-fragility-robin-diangelo.html on August 3, 2020.

Blake, J. (2004). *Shocking photo created a hero, but not to his family.* Accessed at http://edition.cnn.com/2011/US/05/16/Zwerg.freedom.rides/index.html on February 1, 2021.

Boston University. (2020, November 13). *Why do so many parents avoid talking about race?* [News release]. Accessed at www.eurekalert.org/pub_releases/2020-11/bu-wds111320.php on February 8, 2021.

Boyatzis, R., Smith, M., & Van Oosten, E. (2019). *Helping people change: Coaching with compassion for lifelong learning and growth.* Boston: Harvard Business Review Press.

Brown, B. (n.d.). Song from a cotton field. On *Completed recorded works (1925–29).* Scotland: Document Records.

Card, D., & Giuliano, L. (2016, November 15). Universal screening increases the representation of low-income and minority students in gifted education. *Proceedings of the National Academy of Sciences of the United States of America, 113*(48), 13678–13683. Accessed at https://doi.org/10.1073/pnas.1605043113 on February 8, 2021.

Castellano, J. A. (2018). *Educating Hispanic and Latino students: Opening the doors to hope, promise, and possibility.* West Palm Beach, FL: Learning Sciences International.

Cederquist, A., & Golüke, U. (2016). Teaching with scenarios: A social innovation to foster learning and social change in times of great uncertainty. *European Journal of Futures Research, 4*(1), 16–24.

Chowdhury, M. R. (2020, July 28). *What is emotional resilience and how to build it?* Accessed at https://positivepsychology.com /emotional-resilience on August 3, 2020.

Chugh, D. (2018). *The person you mean to be: How good people fight bias.* New York: HarperCollins.

Coates, T-N. (2014, June). The case for reparations. *The Atlantic.* Accessed at www.theatlantic.com/magazine/archive/2014/06/the -case-for-reparations/361631 on August 3, 2020.

Coates, T-N. (2015). *Between the world and me.* New York: Spiegel & Grau.

Cobb, J. (2019, July 3). The Supreme Court just legitimized a cornerstone element of voter suppression. *New Yorker.* Accessed at www.newyorker.com/news/daily-comment/the -supreme-court-just-legitimized-a-cornerstone-element-of-voter -suppression on July 26, 2020.

Cole, D. (2020, July 27). *Tom Cotton describes slavery as a "necessary evil" in bid to keep schools from teaching 1619 Project.* Accessed at www.cnn.com/2020/07/27/politics/tom-cotton -slavery-necessary-evil-1619-project/index.html on July 28, 2020.

Connerly, W. (2020, July 24). America isn't a racist country. *The Wall Street Journal*. Accessed at www.wsj.com/articles/america-isnt-a-racist-country-11595628914 on July 27, 2020.

Craig, L. (2017, April 11). *Racial bias may begin in babies at six months, U of T research reveals*. Accessed at www.utoronto.ca/news/racial-bias-may-begin-babies-six-months-u-t-research-reveals on July 19, 2020.

Culture. (n.d.). In *Merriam-Webster's online dictionary*. Accessed at www.merriam-webster.com/dictionary/culture on January 27, 2021.

da Loba, A. (2013, May 7). At what age should sex education begin? *The New York Times*. Accessed at www.nytimes.com/roomfordebate/2013/05/07/at-what-age-should-sex-education-begin on July 26, 2020.

DiAngelo, R. (2018). *White fragility: Why it's so hard for white people to talk about racism*. Boston: Beacon Press.

Dipto, A. (n.d.). What is modulus of resilience? Calculation & unit. Accessed at https://civiltoday.com/structural-engineering/260-what-is-modulus-of-resilience-calculation-unit on April 24, 2020.

Discussion. (n.d.). In *Merriam-Webster's online dictionary*. Accessed at www.merriam-webster.com/dictionary/discussion on January 27, 2021.

Douglass, F. (1857). *Two speeches by Frederick Douglass; West India emancipation. And the Dred Scott decision*. Rochester, NY: Dewey. Accessed at www.loc.gov/item/mfd.21039 on April 11, 2021.

Dweck, C. S. (2016). *Mindset: The new psychology of success* (Updated ed.). New York: Random House.

Eberhardt, J. L. (2019). *Biased: Uncovering the hidden prejudice that shapes what we see, think, and do*. New York: Viking.

Edmondson, A. C. (2019). *The fearless organization: Creating psychological safety in the workplace for learning, innovation, and growth*. Hoboken, NJ: Wiley.

Elmore, R. F. (Ed.). (2011). *I used to think . . . And now I think . . .: Twenty leading educators reflect on the work of school reform*. Cambridge, MA: Harvard Education Press.

Environmental Protection Agency. (n.d.). *Children's environmental health facts*. Accessed at www.epa.gov/children/childrens -environmental-health-facts on July 26, 2020.

Farnam Street. (n.d.). *Maya Angelou on haters, life, reading, and love* [Blog post]. Accessed at https://fs.blog/2014/09/maya -angelou-on-haters-life-reading-and-love on February 24, 2021.

Flemming, G. (2019, June 3). *The formula to creating safety for any conversation*. Accessed at https://vitalsmarts.com.au/the-formula -to-creating-safety-for-any-conversation on August 3, 2020.

Gardner, H. (1999). *The disciplined mind: What all students should understand*. New York: Simon & Schuster.

Gewertz, C. (2020, April 20). *Exhausted and grieving: Teaching during the coronavirus crisis*. Accessed at www .miamitimesonline.com/covid-19_hub/exhausted-and-grieving -teaching-during-the-coronavirus-crisis/article_d494c94c-8357 -11ea-bcb7-075cf66f7c06.html on May 8, 2020.

Ghandnoosh, N. (2018, June). *How defense attorneys can eliminate racial disparities in criminal justice*. Accessed at www .sentencingproject.org/wp-content/uploads/2018/08/How-Defense -Attorneys-Can-Eliminate-Racial-Disparities-in-Criminal-Justice -System.pdf on July 26, 2020.

Gillard, M. J. (2020, July 7). *Do white people get it? Racism through the eyes of a black male teacher*. Accessed at www.edweek.org /tm/articles/2020/07/07/do-white-people-get-it-racism-through.html on July 26, 2020.

Gladwell, M. (2019). *Talking to strangers: What we should know about the people we don't know*. New York: Little, Brown.

Goldenberg, D. M. (2003). *The curse of Ham: Race and slavery in early Judaism, Christianity, and Islam*. Princeton, NJ: Princeton University Press.

Gopnik, A. (2016, May). *Little scientists: Babies have scientific minds*. Accessed at www.scientificamerican.com/article/little -scientists-babies-have-scientific-minds on August 3, 2020.

Gould, S. J. (1996). *The mismeasure of man* [Rev. ed]. New York: Norton.

Grainger, P. (1927). *Song from a cotton field* [Recorded by Bessie Brown]. Accessed at https://genius.com/Bessie-brown-song-from -a-cotton-field-lyrics on August 3, 2020.

Grant, A. (2021). *Think again: The power of knowing what you don't know.* New York: Viking.

Gupta, N. (2019, June 13). *Students thrown into real-world scenarios with ViewPoint, an educational simulation tool.* Accessed at https://engaged.umich.edu/news-features/students-thrown-into -real-world-scenarios-with-viewpoint-an-educational-simulation -tool on June 29, 2020.

Guskey, T. R. (2020). Flip the script on change: Experience shapes teachers' attitudes and beliefs. *The Learning Professional, 41*(2), 18–22. Accessed at https://learningforward.org/journal/beyond -the-basics/flip-the-script-on-change on August 3, 2020.

Hannah-Jones, N. (2019, August 14). The 1619 Project. *The New York Times.* Accessed at www.nytimes.com/interactive/2019/08/14 /magazine/black-history-american-democracy.html on July 28, 2020.

Harford, T. (2021). *The data detective: Ten easy rules to make sense of statistics.* New York: Riverhead Books.

Harkness, J. (2008). *Hip hop culture and America's most taboo word.* Accessed at https://journals.sagepub.com/doi/pdf/10.1525 /ctx.2008.7.3.38 on July 27, 2020.

Haslam, N. (2017, May 19). *A short history of trigger warnings.* Accessed at https://psychlopaedia.org/society/republished/whats -the-difference-between-traumatic-fear-and-moral-anger-trigger -warnings-wont-tell-you on July 26, 2017.

Hattie, J., & Yates, G. C. R. (2014). *Visible learning and the science of how we learn.* New York: Routledge.

Hauser, C. (2020, June 10). *Merriam-Webster revises "racism" entry after Missouri woman asks for changes.* Accessed at www .nytimes.com/2020/06/10/us/merriam-webster-racism-definition .html on February 19, 2021.

Herrnstein, R. J., & Murray, C. (1996). *The bell curve: Intelligence and class structure in American life.* New York: Simon & Schuster.

Hollie, S. (2017). *Culturally and linguistically responsive teaching and learning: Classroom practices for student success* (2nd ed.). Huntington Beach, CA: Shell Education.

Israel, M. (2015). *From chaos to coherence: Managing stress while teaching.* Accessed at www.educationworld.com/a_admin/admin /admin413.shtml on May 8, 2020.

Jaschik, S. (2019, February 11). *More AP success; racial gaps remain.* Accessed at www.insidehighered.com/admissions /article/2019/02/11/more-students-earn-3-advanced-placement -exams-racial-gaps-remain on June 30, 2020.

Johnson, L. (2014). *Resilience: The art of bouncing back.* Accessed at https://cognitivebehaviortherapycenter.com/resilience on May 7, 2020.

Kang, H-J., Bae, K-Y., Kim, S-W., Shin, H-Y., Shin, I-S., Yoon, J-S., et al. (2017). Impact of anxiety and depression on physical health condition and disability in an elderly Korean population. *Psychiatry Investigation, 14*(3), 240–248.

Kendi, I. X. (2020, July 23). Patience is a dirty word. *The Atlantic.* Accessed at www.theatlantic.com/ideas/archive/2020/07/john -lewis-and-danger-gradualism/614512 on September 8, 2020.

King, A. L., Finnin, M. S., & Kramer, C. M. (2018, July). *Significance of skull fractures and traumatic brain injuries potentially caused by blunt-impact non-lethal weapons.* Accessed at www.ida.org/-/media/feature/publications/s/si /significant-of-skull-fractures-and-traumatic-brain-injuries /significance-of-skull-fractures-and-traumatic-brain-injuries -potentially.ashx on July 27, 2020.

King, M. L., Jr. (2010). *Why we can't wait.* Boston: Beacon Press. (Original work published 1964)

Kinzler, K. (2020). *How you say it: Why you talk the way you do— and what it says about you.* Boston: Houghton Mifflin Harcourt.

Korisko, G. (n.d.). *It's not my fault I never learned to accept responsibility* [Blog post]. Accessed at www.rebootauthentic.com /blog/accept-responsibility on July 19, 2020.

Kristof, N. D., & WuDunn, S. (2019). *Tightrope: Americans reaching for hope.* New York: Knopf.

Landsberg, L. (2013, July 12). *If not now, when?* [Blog post]. Accessed at https://reformjudaism.org/blog/if-not-now-when-0 on February 1, 2021.

Lynch, M. (2016, September 2). *The story of American education and the McGuffey readers.* Accessed at www.theedadvocate.org /story-american-education-mcguffey-readers on July 19, 2020.

Mayo Clinic Staff. (2019, April 4). *Stress management.* Accessed at www.mayoclinic.org/healthy-lifestyle/stress-management /in-depth/stress-symptoms/art-20050987 on May 8, 2020.

McGuffey, W. H. (1879). *McGuffey's fourth eclectic reader* [Rev. ed.]. New York: Wiley. Accessed at www.gutenberg.org /files/14880/14880-pdf.pdf on August 3, 2020.

Meatto, K. (2019, May 2). Still separate, still unequal: Teaching about school segregation and educational inequality. *The New York Times.* Accessed at www.nytimes.com/2019/05/02/learning /lesson-plans/still-separate-still-unequal-teaching-about-school -segregation-and-educational-inequality.html on July 19, 2020.

National Museum of African American History and Culture. (n.d.). *Joe Louis* [Blog post]. Accessed at https://nmaahc.si.edu/blog -post/joe-louis on February 9, 2021.

Nelson, L. (2016, September 21). *Trump calls for nationwide "stop-and-frisk" policy.* Accessed at www.politico.com/story/2016/09 /donald-trump-stop-and-frisk-228486 on July 26, 2020.

The new ideology of race and what is wrong with it. (2020, July 9). *The Economist.* Accessed at www.economist.com/leaders /2020/07/09/the-new-ideology-of-race on July 12, 2020.

Ortiz de Montellano, B. R. (1993). Melanin, Afrocentricity, and pseudoscience. *Yearbook of Physical Anthropology, 36,* 33–58.

Peck, M. S. (2002). *The road less traveled: A new psychology of love, traditional values, and spiritual growth* (25th anniversary ed.). New York: Simon & Schuster. (Original work published 1978)

Poetry Foundation. (n.d.). *Stopping by woods on a snowy evening.* Accessed at www.poetryfoundation.org/poems/42891/stopping-by -woods-on-a-snowy-evening on February 9, 2021.

Racism. (n.d.). In *Merriam-Webster's online dictionary.* Accessed at www.merriam-webster.com/dictionary/racism on February 19, 2021.

Rath, T., & Conchie, B. (2008). *Strengths based leadership: Great leaders, teams, and why people follow.* New York: Gallup Press.

Reeves, D. (Ed.). (2007). *Ahead of the curve: The power of assessment to transform teaching and learning.* Bloomington, IN: Solution Tree Press.

Reeves, D. (2010). *Transforming professional development into student results.* Alexandria, VA: Association for Supervision and Curriculum Development.

Reeves, D. (2019, January 25). *Five skills colleges really want now* [Blog post]. Accessed at www.creativeleadership.net/blog/five-skills-colleges-really-want-now on June 30, 2020.

Reeves, D. (2020). *Achieving equity and excellence: Immediate results from the lessons of high-poverty, high-success schools.* Bloomington, IN: Solution Tree Press.

Reeves, D. (2021). *Deep change leadership: A model for renewing and strengthening schools and districts.* Bloomington, IN: Solution Tree Press.

Reeves, D., & Reeves, B. (2017). *The myth of the muse: Supporting virtues that inspire creativity.* Bloomington, IN: Solution Tree Press.

Saleh, M. (2020, April 9). *A double whammy: The COVID-19 pandemic and burnout in medical professionals.* Accessed at https://leanforward.hms.harvard.edu/2020/04/09/a-double -whammy-the-covid-19-pandemic-and-burnout-in-medical -professionals on May 8, 2020.

Schneider, J. (2020, June 25). Pass-fail raises the question: What's the point of grades? *The New York Times*. Accessed at www.nytimes .com/2020/06/25/opinion/coronavirus-school-grades.html on July 26, 2020.

Shpancer, N. (2010, August 21). *What doesn't kill you makes you weaker* [Blog post]. Accessed at www.psychologytoday.com/us /blog/insight-therapy/201008/what-doesnt-kill-you-makes-you -weaker on August 27, 2020.

Singleton, G. E. (2015). *Courageous conversations about race: A field guide for achieving equity in schools* (2nd ed.). Thousand Oaks, CA: SAGE.

Smith, M. D. (2018, January 18). The truth about "the arc of the moral universe." *The Huffington Post*. Accessed at www.huffpost.com /entry/opinion-smith-obama-king_n_5a5903e0e4b04f3c55a252a4 on July 19, 2020.

Stewart, N. (2020, June 26). Black activists wonder: Is protesting just trendy for white people? *The New York Times*. Accessed at www .nytimes.com/2020/06/26/nyregion/black-lives-matter-white -people-protesters.html on July 10, 2020.

Stoner, K. (2019, October 1). *Science proves that what doesn't kill you makes you stronger.* Accessed at https://news.northwestern .edu/stories/2019/10/science-proves-that-what-doesnt-kill-you -makes-you-stronger on July 27, 2020.

Swift, J. (n.d.). *The curious history of slavery in Africa.* Accessed at https://research.cornell.edu/news-features/curious-history-slavery -west-africa on July 20, 2020.

Thompson, T. (2013, August 21). *NYPD's infamous stop-and-frisk policy found unconstitutional.* Accessed at https://civilrights.org /edfund/resource/nypds-infamous-stop-and-frisk-policy-found -unconstitutional on July 26, 2020.

Valdes, K. S. (2017, March 30). *Role-play as an SEL teaching tool* [Blog post]. Accessed at www.edutopia.org/blog/role-play-sel -teaching-tool-kristin-stuart-valdes on June 30, 2020.

Wiseman, L. (2017). *Multipliers: How the best leaders make everyone smarter* (Rev. and updated ed.). New York: Harper Business.

Ye, B. (2018, May 4). *Why I take responsibility for things that aren't my fault*. Accessed at https://byrslf.co/why-i-take-responsibility -for-things-that-arent-my-fault-9eb3b377e3b5 on July 19, 2020.

Yiu, Y. (2020, March 18). *Visualizing Twitter echo chambers*. Accessed at www.insidescience.org/news/visualizing-twitter-echo -chambers on July 10, 2020.

Index

Achieving Equity and Excellence
Douglas Reeves
Achieve high performance for all in your school. In this book, Douglas Reeves shares the mindset of high-poverty, high-success schools and outlines how to follow their example to make dramatic improvements to student learning, behavior, and attendance in a single semester.
BKF928

Transforming School Culture
Anthony Muhammad
Muhammad describes the prevailing beliefs and assumptions of four different types of educators: Believers, Fundamentalists, Tweeners, and Survivors. After arguing that their collective dynamic ultimately determines the culture of a school, he provides specific strategies for working with each group.
BKF793

Overcoming the Achievement Gap Trap
Anthony Muhammad
Ensure learning equality in every classroom. Investigate previous and current policies designed to help close the achievement gap. Explore strategies for adopting a new mindset that frees educators and students from negative academic performance expectations.
BKF618

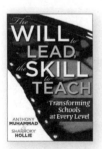

The Will to Lead, the Skill to Teach
Anthony Muhammad and Sharroky Hollie
The authors acknowledge both the structural and sociological issues that contribute to low-performing schools and offer multiple tools and strategies to assess and improve classroom management, increase literacy, establish academic vocabulary, and contribute to a healthier school culture.
BKF443

Solution Tree | Press

Visit SolutionTree.com or call 800.733.6786 to order.